CREATE AND ORCHESTRATE

CREATE AND ORCHESTRATE

THE PATH TO CLAIMING YOUR CREATIVE POWER FROM AN UNLIKELY ENTREPRENEUR

MARCUS WHITNEY

CREATE AND ORCHESTRATE

The Path to Claiming Your Creative Power
from an Unlikely Entrepreneur

ISBN   978-1-5445-0978-5 *Hardcover*
       978-1-5445-0977-8 *Paperback*
       978-1-5445-0976-1 *Ebook*

*To Isabel and John Whitney, I am who I am because
of you. Every child should be so lucky.*

*To Tristan and Ciaran Whitney, I lived up to what I could
be because of you. Every father should be so lucky.*

*To Rachel Whitney, I healed and became whole
again because of you. No husband is luckier.*

CONTENTS

A NOTE FROM THE AUTHOR

MARCH 23, 2020

Thank you for reading this book.

I began writing this book in 2015. Between 2015 and 2019, many things in my life changed, personally and professionally, for the better. There were of course trials, but overall during that time, I prospered in business and well-being.

As we entered 2020, I was incredibly excited to finally get this book out into the world.

I was supposed to turn in the absolute final manuscript on March 10. But I didn't, because I was rearranging my house to serve as a home office and production studio as I began my own self-instructed "stay at home" order at the dawn of the COVID-19 epidemic in the United States. The next day the World Health Organization declared COVID-19 a global pandemic.

I knew that before I submitted the manuscript for publishing, I needed to include a note to you about the fact that I wrote a book about entrepreneurship during the back half of the 2010s because obviously the world will be very different in the 2020s.

No one really knows how things are going to be after COVID-19.

But one thing I believe with all my heart is that we will rebuild our world in time.

So, I submit *Create and Orchestrate* as one of many tools we may use in the rebuilding. We will need brave, clever entrepreneurs to dust themselves off and create new value to revive our economy and solve the problems we find ourselves threatened by. We will need innovators to bolster our global health system to ensure we are much better prepared the next time an infectious disease threatens millions of our lives.

My sincere hope is that this book helps prepare those souls.

I wish you health, clarity of purpose, and the courage to believe.

Marcus

FOREWORD

Anyone who has ever hired people at startups knows how tricky it is. You're essentially trying to decide if this person you barely know is going to be a perfect fit for a job that's inevitably going to change over time in a company that's going to change even more quickly, all based on a couple of coffee meetings, some of the best (but still not very good) interview questions you can come up with, and ultimately, a gut feeling—a hunch.

And then once in a long while, you meet someone like Marcus, which I did way back in September 2003. My good friend, Will Weaver, and I were building out the team at our email marketing software company called Emma, one of the early (and few) software companies in Nashville at that time. And we were pretty much running the entire thing on hunches, having never started or grown a company before.

We were, in the parlance of startups, completely and utterly winging it. And so hunches were important. And when we met Marcus over coffee that day in September, our hunchometers were going off like crazy.

And it wasn't just because he seemed to have some of the experience we needed in a software engineer. Marcus also had something much more important—he had *it*. You know, *it*. That inherently indefinable quality that makes you immediately want to sign up for whatever the It Person is doing, building, or selling. And Marcus is just one of those It People. We hired him as quickly as we could, figuring that he might be a pretty good engineer, but he was no doubt the kind of curious, charismatic, compelling It Person we wanted in our world.

And yet, it was pretty clear from the start that Emma was just one stop on a long creative journey for Marcus. He was always destined to go out and launch his own things, build his own platforms, and ultimately become his own platform. Because Marcus was always somehow bigger than whatever thing Marcus happened to be doing at the time. Even during Emma's super-early days, he found a way to play up a level or two—he ended up running all of engineering and becoming a core part of our leadership team. Before we knew it, he took us to South by Southwest when that was a relatively new thing, he helped launch events like BarCamp back home that brought the entire software and creative communities together. You name it—he never seemed to be overly concerned with or constrained by his current place and time.

And so of course, all these years later, Marcus has eventually gotten around to writing a book about his creative life journey. And he's on the cover because it would be weird to have someone else's face on a book by and about Marcus. You should totally read it—wait, you already are! Well done. Long after we stopped being everyday colleagues, Marcus and I have continued to grab coffee to talk about life and career, the startup world, the nonstartup world most normal humans inhabit, kids and the challenges of raising them (okay, mostly that last thing). And I can promise you that as much as you'll enjoy reading this book, you'll enjoy getting to know the man behind the book even more. Just please, please don't challenge the guy on the cover to a jiu-jitsu match. Call it a hunch.

Enjoy the read,

Clint Smith
Co-founder and former CEO of Emma
Nearly twenty-year friend of Marcus Whitney

CHAPTER ONE

• • •

DON'T BELIEVE THE HYPE

AN INTRODUCTION AND AN INVITATION

Listen carefully.

There is a universal language in the world today and it isn't English or Chinese. The universal language of our world is business. While we have not all agreed on whose God is right or what laws we should live by, every developed nation has agreed to exchange money for value.

Understanding the universal language of business is challenging for two reasons. First, the education you received in school has not made it a priority. Second, like most languages, to truly learn it, you have to practice it.

The universal language of business is no different than

any other language in one very important way: you do not need credentials or anyone's approval to speak it. And just like learning a new language, understanding business will give you the ability to see the world in an entirely new way. Understanding the language of business is power.

There are a lot of books on business. So what makes this one different?

This book is about entrepreneurship, written by an entrepreneur, who learned business by doing it. Entrepreneurship is the art and science of achieving sustainable business growth. Entrepreneurship is a vehicle for your creativity. When practiced, entrepreneurship enables you to express yourself through your business. Entrepreneurship creates agency and leverage to impact the world at scale. Entrepreneurship can supercharge you.

This book is action-oriented. It is a practitioner's perspective. Through my story and the learnings derived from my experiences, you will see that you can achieve many of your goals and dreams through business. My intent is to encourage you to use entrepreneurship to level the playing field for yourself and those you care about and to make the world a more fair and equitable place. You have the power and the opportunity to change the world.

THE CHALLENGE OF OUR BRAVE NEW WORLD

The technologies that transformed the world have obscured the path to a good living. The internet, mobile phones, and the tech titans' (Amazon, Google, Apple, Facebook, etc.) relentless pursuit of perfecting customer experience has killed many industry incumbents while giving birth to new ones. Those of us who don't understand how to leverage technology are finding it harder to make ends meet.

In the United States, our political, criminal justice, education, and healthcare systems all favor the wealthy. We talk about the 1 percent and the inequity it represents, but no one seems to have a good plan for leveling the playing field. While the technologies of the twenty-first century have lowered the barriers to launch a business, they have not resulted in a significant rebalance of power. In fact, by many measures, power is only getting more imbalanced.

The new economic mode of the world is "rapid change." A viable skill today may not be viable in ten years. You now must read trends and forecast change so you can benefit from it rather than suffer because of it. You need to be able to think and move like an entrepreneur, even in how you navigate your career. Unfortunately, entrepreneurship has been hyped up by the media to be something inaccessible to many who don't have the right education, background, and connections.

The book in your hands has been designed to shatter that narrative.

I am going to illuminate a path to your power through entrepreneurship. In this book, I provide you with a framework for the fundamental concepts that every business on Earth relies upon. I give you a cheat sheet for one of the most misunderstood forces in the business world today, Venture Capital (VC). Through my experiences, successes, and failures alike, I share important and unintuitive principles for founders to operate by. Most importantly, I prove that entrepreneurship is accessible to you at all levels as long as you are patient and willing to put in the work.

You may not be ready to make the leap into entrepreneurship yet, and that's fine. But make no mistake, it's almost impossible to understand the massive shifts you are seeing in the world today if you don't understand how entrepreneurship works. Entrepreneurship is not just for startups. The most valuable and dominant companies in the world today are entrepreneurial at their core, and the rules of the new economy say that if you want to be competitive, you have to be too.

THE MOMENT THAT MADE ME WRITE THIS BOOK

In March 2015, I met a woman named Karen Vander Molen, who founded the BEST program in Nashville, Tennessee.

BEST stands for Building Entrepreneurs for Success in Tennessee, and the entrepreneurs it seeks to build are incarcerated. The BEST program provides opportunities for personal development and transformation and teaches business and entrepreneurial skills to better equip people for successful reentry into society. Karen asked me to tell my story about finding success and happiness as an entrepreneur to a cohort of nineteen women at the Tennessee Prison for Women.

As I drove up to the prison, the reality of where I was sunk in. As I looked up, I could see cameras on poles and as I looked ahead, I saw no other cars on the road. There was a quiet uneasiness in the air as I parked, got out of my car, and started the long walk towards the heavily gated, nondescript building. Cell phones were not allowed in the prison, so I brought my printed instructions on what to do when I got to the visitor's station. As I entered the facility and walked up to the desk to get signed in, my heart raced. Even though the process was designed to ensure the safety of visitors, I did not feel safe. It was impossible to ignore that this place was managing the ever-present potential of danger.

I signed all the appropriate paperwork, passed through the metal detector, and was escorted down several corridors before arriving at a door that looked like the exterior of a public school classroom. The escort opened the door and Karen was there to greet me. She then introduced me to the women of BEST and let them know that I would be telling them about my entrepreneurial journey.

I walked to the front of the room and looked at the women, attentive and engaged, took a deep breath...and began to share my story.

BUT FOR THE GRACE

In 1993 at age seventeen, I was enrolled as a freshman at the University of Virginia's School of Architecture. That year was also the beginning of the "Golden Era" of hip-hop, and I wanted nothing more than to be a part of it. I was much more interested in the lyrics of Nas, The Notorious B.I.G. and Wu-Tang than the history of the Lancet Arch. My friend and I started a hip-hop group together, and the three key ingredients for an aspiring rapper back then were writing rhymes, making beats, and smoking weed. None of those things are conducive to success in one of the most competitive architecture schools in the country.

Fast forward to 1996, and I graduated from regular weed smoker to amateur weed peddler in order to keep a steady supply around me for songwriting and recording sessions. Here I was, a student at one of the top universities in the country, throwing a precious opportunity away because I was too immature to appreciate it. The University predictably suspended me. My desire to become a rap star led me to become an accidental drug dealer instead of getting the degree I went to Charlottesville for. My first entrepreneurial endeavor was neither smart nor legal.

My friend and I both found ourselves unenrolled due to our failure to attend classes, so we decided to move to Fairfax in Northern Virginia where his older brother lived. We continued our lifestyle of hip-hop and weed selling in an apartment there. One evening at the apartment while hanging out with some friends, partying, and playing music too loud, there was a knock at the door. When my friend's older brother went to see who was at the door, someone kicked it open. Before we could blink, there were eight men dressed in all black with ski masks and guns pulled on us.

I thought I was going to die.

But fortunately, we weren't being robbed. They were cops, and this was a raid. I was in a police drug raid.

Lucky for me, there was not much illegal inventory in the apartment during the raid and I avoided being charged. Had they chosen to raid the apartment on a different day, the rest of my life could have been much different. I never sold drugs again, and I've committed to making money legally since that day.

After I shared my story with the women of the BEST program, they knew I understood from my own experiences that they weren't inherently bad people, they just made a mistake and were paying for it. For many of them, those mistakes happened before they were twenty-one years old.

These women were truly excited about entrepreneurship, holding onto a dream of what they would do with their new knowledge of business when the State of Tennessee granted them their freedom. **One woman told me that she had never heard the word "entrepreneur" until she was told about the BEST program.** When she said that, it atomized any idea I had that the word entrepreneur is played out or overused—that's only true for those who live in the entrepreneurial echo chamber. A significant segment of people in the US don't understand what entrepreneurship is or that it is a possibility for them.

ENTREPRENEURSHIP IS THE GREAT EQUALIZER

Horace Mann, a celebrated American educational reformer who advocated for public education in the 1800s said, "Education then, beyond all other devices of human origin, **is the great equalizer** of the conditions of men, the balance wheel of the social machinery." I agree with Mann in the context of the twentieth century, but things change. I believe that in the twenty-first century, entrepreneurship is replacing education as the great equalizer of power among people in free and democratic societies.

The core of Mann's statement is not about education, it's about learning valuable knowledge and skills. Both education and entrepreneurship are models for learning. Education, as we know it today, refers to academia; it is often theoretical, simulated, and taking place in an academy setting. Entrepreneurship is a real-world, experiential model of learning.

Entrepreneurship is responsible for the creation of the wealthiest and most powerful people in the United States, and this is becoming increasingly true of most countries in the developed world. While higher education can serve as a booster for success, it is not a requirement for entrepreneurship. I do not intend to persuade people to avoid formal higher education. But I do have a message for those who believe higher education is not the universal answer. Entrepreneurship excludes no one.

When people promote entrepreneurship, it often comes with a warning about the risks to one's financial, mental, and emotional health. It's true, all of those risks exist in entrepreneurship. But why don't we talk as much about the risks of student debt and the decreasing return on investment that a bachelor's degree has had over the last twenty-five years? Why don't we seek to decrease the severity of the risks of entrepreneurship through mentorship, training, and community?

Higher education is a mega-industry and would disrupt

itself if it was more honest about its inability to keep up with the pace of change in the world. Our society refuses to balance and compare risks between higher education and alternative paths. This results in a significant segment of our population being guilted into attending college in an era where they have more optionality than ever. Openly questioning the merit of higher education comes at great risk to one's reputation, and that is a risk very few people of influence will accept.

This hypocrisy is part of what drove me to write this book. Entrepreneurship is accessible to you, and I wanted to do what I could to help make it more accessible. I encourage you to explore entrepreneurship, and I'm sharing the lessons I've learned to decrease your risk should you decide to try it. If you are already on this path, I hope to help you walk it with more confidence and clarity.

AMBITIOUS, CREATIVE REBELS

Let's take a second to talk about risk and how we frame it in society when we educate and raise children. When raising children, we don't project the same risk prevention messaging we do around entrepreneurship as we do in other more risky paths in life...like athletics. We don't pull children out of little league sports just because the chances of them going to the pros from high school are less than 1 percent. That's because we understand that even if our children don't become professional athletes, that doesn't mean the training they received in little league was worthless. We believe they will take the lessons they learn in sports into other areas of their lives, and those lessons will have lasting value.

What if using that same logic, we taught all children how to be entrepreneurs? Even if they didn't become entrepreneurs, they could still use what they learned in their training and apply it to whatever path of life they chose. How much more prepared would they be for disruption in their industry if they understood why disruption exists and could see it coming?

Growing up, I didn't know what an entrepreneur was, even though I was raised by one. My mom left her job while I was in high school to start a medical billing business with one of her best friends. I didn't understand that what she was doing professionally was an option for me. While my mother influenced my future at a subconscious level, her example didn't eliminate my own self-doubts about becoming an entrepreneur. Was I doing the right thing? Was I even a good person being so rogue in my choices?

In reflection, my personality led me to relentlessly pursue entrepreneurship once I found it. My ambitious and rebellious nature, which could have gotten me in a lot of trouble in life, are the traits that made me relentlessly pursue entrepreneurship. I always thought I had a better way to do something.

Many people are ambitious, creative rebels who could change the world if they only knew how. Ambitious, creative rebels like Steve Jobs, Mark Zuckerberg, and Jeff Bezos. Under different circumstances, these remarkable innovators with rebellious personalities could have ended up in prison just like the women I met in the BEST program.

When I stood in front of those women, I knew sharing my story would become part of my purpose for living. I knew I had to share what I learned from my experiences, regardless of how embarrassing it was. That day in a Tennessee prison catalyzed a belief in me that it's not my job to decide who is cut out to be an entrepreneur and who isn't. It's my job to spread the word about the power entrepreneurship offers and let those who hear the word use it in whatever way best helps them.

I BELIEVE IN YOU

Like the women in the BEST program, you provide me with great hope. I believe you can claim your Creative Power and help bring balance to the world with your gifts. The premise of *Create and Orchestrate* is that Creative Power is accessible to us all. It's part of being human. Entrepreneurship is this era's most effective path to accessing it to a sustainable end.

Create and Orchestrate is about **claiming your Creative Power through entrepreneurship.** Whether your goal is to create a better life for you and your family, to evolve how your government serves its constituents, or to reinvigorate a stale corporation, using your **Creative Power** is a key ingredient in achieving your goals. You can access your Creative Power through different methods, but few are as sustainable as entrepreneurship. This book is a tour behind the entrepreneurial curtain so you can better understand how Creative Power is being leveraged in this era.

I see a future where most of the world's population believes they can be entrepreneurs and have the tools to do so. This era of rapid change, important problems to solve, and democratized access to technology makes that future possible. If you share this vision, then we're partners in this movement. Thanks for being brave enough to bet on yourself.

CHAPTER TWO

* * *

FROM WAITING TABLES TO WRITING CODE

A CHAPTER ABOUT REINVENTING YOURSELF

Being an entrepreneur is living from a position of power. With that power comes responsibility. There is no one to pass blame onto; the buck always stops with you. Things ultimately won't work for you if you aren't consistent in your mind with the goals that come out of your mouth. Creating alignment within yourself is a long process. In this chapter, I'll walk you through how I uncovered the values that enabled me to first understand what creative power feels like.

RETREAT

Becoming an entrepreneur was not a foregone conclusion for me. After spiraling out of control from my failed attempt at a bachelor's degree at the University of Virginia, I went back home to Brooklyn with my tail between my legs to find my footing. Returning to my family as a failure after all they had invested in me to make it to college was a humbling experience. I was young and ambitious, but the reality that I wouldn't be a hip-hop star or an architect had set in.

I will never forget one moment from that experience. I was downstairs in the guest apartment, where my parents let me camp out so I could have some amount of privacy. My dad came downstairs and sat me down at the small kitchen table. For some reason, the light in the kitchen felt like a spotlight in an interrogation room. My dad looked at me with eyes that shifted between sad and outraged, and he just said, "I can't believe you wasted that opportunity. You need to get your life together."

I felt absolutely awful.

My parents were obviously disappointed, but they never stopped loving me and believing in me, and that was an incredible lesson. Their unconditional love at this shameful moment showed me that failure is not final.

Going home proved helpful for resetting my sense of self. After three years away, I came back to the home I was raised in my entire life, to watch my parents live their lives on a day-to-day basis. What I took for granted before I left for college, but now could clearly see, was the incredible work ethic both my parents had.

Neither of my parents graduated from college. They both worked during my entire life (and before I was even thought of), always keeping a job, investing their middle-class wages into my future. My father worked some of the hardest jobs out there. He was a corrections officer in New York, he worked in construction, and he worked in the clearinghouse for the United States Postal Service. On top of all this, he always worked the night shift.

I didn't get to the University of Virginia on my own. My parents dedicated their lives to make sure I went to a great private school for junior high and high school and was prepared to attend college. Being in their presence again, receiving their love and forgiveness inspired me to adopt the first of my entrepreneurial values—hard work.

As healing as returning home was, living under my parents' roof at twenty-one years old would not work for long. It was only a matter of time before I moved out. While my time in Virginia wasn't ideal, I did grow accustomed to the weather and hospitality of the Southeast US. At the same time, coming home to New York reminded me that I felt most alive and motivated in a city environment. With this criteria in mind, there was one logical place for me to make my next home: Atlanta, Georgia.

RELAUNCH, WORK HARD

In Atlanta, I re-engaged my creative side as a spoken word artist, performing at various venues around the city to local acclaim which helped my self-confidence. When I wasn't performing, I worked nonstop—waiting tables at various restaurants or as a phone jockey at a few collection agencies. I enjoyed waiting tables because I liked serving people and being rewarded for the quality of service I provided. I liked the collections job because I could help people figure out ways to resolve their debt. Most people didn't know they had options (or even consumer rights), and I enjoyed educating them and helping to get them on a path to resolution.

I met a woman while at one of those collection agencies, and a month after we met, we were a couple and I was fired for inability to focus on my job. Within a year we got married and started a family. There's nothing like being married at twenty-four without a college degree, with one child and another on the way to make you think about your life differently. As we talked about our situation, we decided Atlanta wasn't an ideal long-term home for our family. With no reason other than it being the city where she went to high school and still having a close friend who lived there, we packed up everything we owned and drove from Atlanta to Nashville, Tennessee.

Little did I know then that Nashville would become the canvas upon which I would create the person I am today.

On Labor Day of the year 2000, we arrived in Nashville and drove down the central street of the city's downtown neighborhood, Broadway, to get a feel for our new home. As you head west away from Downtown, Broadway turns into West End, and on West End, there was a Mexican restaurant called Rio Bravo Cantina, a happy-hour hangout for college kids and young professionals. This was the same chain I worked at in Atlanta, and I happened to be wearing my Rio Bravo uniform as we drove into town.

I walked in the restaurant, and because it was Labor Day, they were slammed. I walked up to the manager (I knew how they dressed) and said I was new to town and would like to work there if they had any openings. He asked if I was in the company's system, and I said yes. Then he said, "You're in section five, go!" I went back to my car, told my wife to find a place to stay, and started work on my first day in Nashville.

A week later, I found out there was another chain restaurant in Nashville that I had worked at in Atlanta, a brunch spot called Le Peep. I'd get hired there as well, working

Monday through Friday at Rio Bravo, and weekends at Le Peep. We'd landed in Nashville and right away, I was able to pay for the efficiency hotel room in Bellevue that my wife scouted out. So far, so good in Nashville.

Le Peep was in Belle Meade, which I would later learn was the neighborhood of Nashville's wealthiest families. This turned out to be important in the coming months, but I'll get to that later. The two gigs provided enough cash to keep my family afloat, but every passing day was one day closer to our second child being born. Our expenses were about to increase, and things were getting real.

I felt pressure every day to get healthcare coverage, be at home more to help my pregnant wife with our one-year-old, and stabilize income. Waiting tables is a game of highs and lows. Some days are great, and you can go home with hundreds of dollars in your pocket. Some days literally generate no money. The days where I brought home little to no money were super stressful, and I dreaded going home to report to my wife. I couldn't just stay here; I needed to find a better way to make money.

The answer for me was not to start a business. I was in no position to do that; I couldn't stop working the long hours at the restaurant to make every dollar I could. What I needed was a better paying job, fast. But there was no clear path to getting a better paying job fast.

I was new in town, I didn't have a network I could leverage, and I had no credentials or skills that would earn me a better paying job. Necessity is the mother of invention, and in my mind, I needed to find a way out of this situation.

BE CLEVER, FIND YOUR OWN LANE

My late uncle Otis was a programmer at IBM in Upstate New York, and for Christmas when I was nine years old, he gave me a PC Jr. It wasn't a successful computer in terms of sales; I was the only kid I knew who had one. The PC Jr. was a big gray plastic block with a keyboard. It could show sixteen colors and only had sixty-four kilobytes of memory. Hard to even imagine how this computer could do anything today, but in the early eighties, the PC Jr. was a magic machine.

Back then, computers didn't do much that you didn't program them to do. You had to learn some basic programming (as I did in a programming language called BASIC) in order to make computers useful or even remotely entertaining. I never learned a foreign language as a child but on that PC Jr., I learned a programming language and the basic principles of how computers work.

In 2000, after society survived the Y2K apocalypse and was riding high on the internet boom, computer programming became a skill that could result in serious economic mobility. Most people didn't consider it possible to leverage that skill to increase your income without a college degree. But I decided that the fastest path to upgrading my income was to figure out how to get a job as a computer programmer without a college degree. I needed to create a strategy to achieve that goal. The first step in the strategy was to begin to learn what programming was like in the first year of the twenty-first century.

I would spend as much free time as I could at Borders bookstore (they're out of business now thanks to Amazon) walking around for hours, treating it like a library. There were rows of books, spines about four to six inches thick with the same font, brandishing titles like ASP, LDAP, JAVA, C++ and PERL. How would I know which of these I needed to read? The answer is: I didn't.

I pulled book after book off the shelf, thumbing through them before committing to one I would purchase. The World Wide Web was the technology of the day in 2000, and one word kept coming up every time I looked for guidance on programing on the web: JavaScript. I bought my first book on JavaScript in the fall of 2000.

Through a connection made by my wife's best friend, I became friends with an IT professional named Eddie. Eddie was a hacker. By day he kept his employer's computer networks secure, and by night he played video games, experimented with ways to break into networks, and collected pirated software for fun. Eddie helped me navigate the never-ending shorthand of the modern computer world and gave me CD after CD of illegal software that I used to develop my skills. Eddie was the best.

I practiced programming every day, but without a real-world project, I never knew if I was getting good enough to get hired by anyone. After a complicated C-section while giving birth to our first son, my wife wanted to give birth to our second son naturally. That was a high-risk proposition, and we needed an experienced midwife to help us make that happen. Of course, we didn't have health insurance or any money to speak of, so we couldn't afford one.

My wife persisted and found the midwife that she wanted. During our initial consultation, we got really excited about how she could help us. Then she quoted her price and my heart sank. Two thousand dollars. There was no way we could afford it. Before I could even think about what I was saying, I asked her if she was happy with her website. She stopped, smiled, and said, "I really need a new website." Five minutes later, we shook hands on a barter deal. I would build our midwife a shiny new website in exchange for her taking us on as clients.

This was a game changer. I built my first website as a pro, and even though I didn't get paid for it, programming started to make life for my family better. That website served as the primary portfolio piece that I used for the next four months while applying for junior software developer positions across Nashville. The day after our youngest son was born, I got the call I had worked so hard for. I was offered a professional programmer job on April 9, 2001 at a continuing education company in the healthcare industry called HealthStream.

People who seek to make a similar transition to the one I made from waiter to employed computer programmer in just eight months always ask me how I did it. First, it's important to acknowledge that I had a background in programming that started at age nine. Even though I was rusty, the experience and familiarity with the world of programming was there. I just had to dig it up and polish it off with hard work.

In between visits to my tables, while orders for my customers were being prepared in the kitchen to be served, I had my computer books from Borders open and was studying. After working *doubles*—shifts that lasted twelve hours—I went home and put in another four hours at the computer working through practice drills.

I spent the little free time I did have on the weekends at the bookstore reading computer books I couldn't afford and taking notes to bring home and practice later in the day. I utilized all the time I had available to me to advance my learning. And I have to acknowledge that my wife was a great partner through this process, allowing me to focus on software by caring for our one-year-old while she was pregnant.

But there was more to it than just hard work. My mindset was critical. Most of my coworkers at the two restaurants I worked at didn't demonstrate the same aspirations that I did. That's not to say they weren't supportive of my efforts, because they were. They always encouraged me to keep studying and asked me how the job hunt was going while I was sending out what felt like hundreds of resumes. However, there wasn't a lot of evidence around me that I could be successful in making this transition. I had to create a mind state supportive of my endeavor.

I didn't achieve that mind state by believing I was becoming a programmer. I achieved that mind state by believing *I already was a programmer*. This distinction is very important. By believing I already was a programmer, even though it wasn't obvious to others, I bypassed many of the limiting thoughts and doubts about my ability to become a programmer. I never said I was a great or even a good programmer. I just believed I was a programmer. This small tweak of believing we already are what we want to be rather than becoming it has significant downstream effects.

With this belief in place, the key to success came down to relentless practice.

In 2020, if you want to become a computer programmer, there are endless methods to do so outside of a four-year college degree. Online classes, both free and paid, six-month boot camps, YouTube channels, and specialized tutors all exist to help aspiring programmers gain the skills they need to become employable. Even with all these opportunities to develop one's skills as a programmer, the demand for talent for these jobs in America continues to outpace the supply of programmers.

When I went from waiter to programmer in the year 2000, this push in society to train people to become computer programmers without degrees didn't exist. A college degree was the only clear path to a career as a programmer. All of society's signals told me I had no business trying to be a professional programmer as a college dropout. If I didn't first bypass those signals and work in every free moment to become good enough to be hired, I never would have achieved my goal.

BUT WHAT IF I'M AFRAID?

Everything I just talked about is great, but what do you do when you are afraid to believe in your ability to do something that your environment tells you isn't possible? What happens when fear prevents you from reinventing yourself? When fear emerges, you have to process it and determine whether it's rational or it's presenting you with an opportunity for growth.

At times your fears will make you aware of legitimate danger ahead in your quest for self-innovation. Some decisions can cause you damage if made incorrectly, so you should beware of harboring *irrational, unsafe beliefs*. Fear can make you aware of risk. You need to look at risk with sober eyes. The risks associated with reinvention can fall into several categories, a few of which are: losing relationships with others, losing who you are, and losing your financial stability.

LOSING RELATIONSHIPS WITH OTHERS

It is often said in circles of self-help that we are the sum of the people we spend the most time with. We learn by observing others, and that includes interactions and observations of the people we're close to. When you endeavor to reinvent yourself, you must adopt some new behaviors and shed some old ones. When you change how you act, some people will celebrate those changes and may join you in changing some of their own behaviors. Others may not respond so well.

If you are feeling fear that as you reinvent yourself, you and some of the people close to you are drifting apart, pay attention. It very well could be happening. Some relationships will not survive your journey. If the relationship cannot afford to be neglected, it will require some increased communication on your part to keep things intact.

LOSING WHO YOU ARE

When you change things about yourself like earning capacity, technical acumen, and social status, you are also likely to experience a change in other aspects of your life. Areas of concern for unhealthy change are your character, your integrity, and your personality. Within these areas, it is important to remain honest with yourself. Trusted friends, mentors, and significant others can be a good barometer for how well you are maintaining your moral compasses as you reinvent yourself.

It's important to come to terms with the fact that transformation is not isolated to one area of our life. There is a fantastic opportunity to have a compound benefit from your efforts to change across multiple areas if you do so consciously. You are always a work in progress. Just as you are developing new skills to enhance your career, you can also enhance your character. I've always found that I can change a bad habit if I replace it with a good habit. However, if I try to change a bad habit by just stopping, I almost always fail. The void left by the bad habit needs to be filled.

If I don't fill the void intentionally, either the same bad habit or a new one will emerge to fill the void.

The same is true of your commitment to stay grounded and become a better person as you develop your expertise. While it's tempting to drop your guard on character development, working on your character while working on a new expertise has amazing returns. If you become a better person while growing your skills, you fast-track your opportunity to become a leader. Working on yourself before you push into entrepreneurship will work to your advantage. Character matters.

LOSING YOUR FINANCIAL STABILITY

Reinvention in the context of work generally means a career change. Even though you're doing this to better your financial situation, the process brings uncertainty as you move away from your current income base. The risk of financial loss can undermine all your good intentions if not properly managed. Never underestimate the loss of focus that not being able to pay your bills will introduce in your life. As you chart your path to your new profession, make sure not to be so impatient that you ultimately delay your process due to going broke.

I've just covered three rational fears and some things to consider as you try to work through them. Many fears, however, are irrational and mostly expose a lack of confidence in your abilities. For these fears, developing a belief in yourself is the only sustainable remedy.

BELIEF IS REQUIRED

The most powerful action you can take in the world to manifest something is to believe in it.

Belief activates your brain. When you believe something, you generate activity in your prefrontal cortex. The prefrontal cortex manages your experience of emotions, rewards, and self-representation. Whether the nature of your belief is religious or about how you see yourself, the act of believing triggers the same effect in your brain. Belief unleashes your Creative Power, and like any tool, its use can be constructive or destructive. Focus on constructive uses of belief to manifest your vision through consistent hard work.

Note: Many of us have experienced trauma in life that may have an override on our ability to activate belief on our own behalf in a positive way. If you don't process and address your trauma, you can't believe something that the trauma is blocking. I don't deal with how to address trauma in this book, but you must deal with it before using belief the way I'm describing in this chapter.

The words "I believe in my heart" have the power to remove

the fear of something and replace your fear with a trust that something is true. Nothing in this book is more important than this: **You must hold a deep belief in your ability to become successful, or you will face at least twice the resistance on your path to achievement.** Belief in yourself is a necessary ingredient to becoming who you want to be. It doesn't make obstacles to your success go away. Rather, it fuels your resilience and commitment to overcome the challenges you will face.

You are the ultimate judge on what is OK to believe in and what isn't. This is your responsibility, and no one else's. As a general rule, if a belief will not be harmful to others or result in you disregarding your personal safety, then it's worth considering. Your intent behind the belief is what matters most. My core belief in 2000 was that I was a programmer. This was a binary decision—either I would see myself as a programmer or I wouldn't. Who else could qualify me as a programmer but me?

By choosing that belief, the world around me made less and less sense as I waited tables and more and more sense as I inched toward my first programming job. *It's this dynamic of our outside world resonating with our internal beliefs that makes believing in being that which we desire to be so powerful.* Others will try to qualify your belief in yourself, and that can be tricky to navigate. It's wise to keep such beliefs to yourself until they become clear and undeniable to the rest of the world. *You will know when that happens as people refer to you and what you believe yourself to be without you having to tell them what you are.*

Pro Tip: Do not self-qualify. Do not focus on what milestones you would have to achieve to be the thing you are working towards. If you are using belief to bypass fear and self-doubt, you are in the early stages of your journey of self-innovation. Using descriptors like "aspiring," "entry-level," and "one day" aren't helpful and negate your belief as far as your brain is concerned. Keep it simple and be the thing you want to be with no qualifying statements.

Bottom line: belief is a tool, not just something that happens to you. You can use it to your advantage to get out of your own way. At least half the time, our own irrational fear is stopping us from becoming who we want to be.

FINDING BALANCE DURING REINVENTION

The question of work-life balance is one that becomes more and more universal as society increases its connection between perceived worth and career. There is a theory regarding work-life balance called the "*Four Burners Theory*," most often credited to a *New Yorker* article by David Sedaris. The theory uses a stove as a metaphor and assigns burners to major areas of life: family, friends, health, and work. The theory says that "to be successful, you have to cut off one of your burners. And in order to be really successful, you have to cut off two." The stove will work with all four burners turned on, but how will your "dishes" turn out if you're switching focus among cooking four things at the same time?

This book is about work, so let's just assume that you will not turn the "work" burner off. How then should you think about the Four Burners Theory when reinventing yourself? I can't answer that for you definitively, but I can say in my experience there is some truth to this theory. When I think about my period of reinvention from waiter to programmer, the first burner I turned on low was the "friend" burner. If you weren't a coworker or someone helping me grow as a programmer, I probably didn't spend much time with you.

Without your health, it's hard to achieve greatness in anything, so you should endeavor to keep that burner well-lit no matter what.

The rub seems to always come in with family. If you're single, then this is easier for you. If you're married and/or have children, this gets more difficult. According to the theory, you only need to cut off one burner to be successful. If you limit your time and energy with friends, you can better achieve your goals with work, your family, and your health.

I've found that the most valuable aspect of this theory is an awareness that the four burners exist. You may reject the idea that you need to cut off any of these burners. However, there is value in setting the expectation of sacrifice as you strive to reinvent and level up your life. Knowing health, family, and friends are the categories to balance, you can be conscious in the process rather than wondering why these areas of your life are suffering.

HUSTLER, HACKER, HERO

It always helps to have a mnemonic to make the recall of critical information easy. For me, there are many things that I will learn and may forget over time, but I never want to forget the core values I learned during this difficult reinvention period. These values have been the constant in my life for the last two decades that have never failed me, especially over the last twelve years of nonstop entrepreneurship.

My slogan for these three values is *Hustler, Hacker, Hero*:

1. **Hustler: *Work hard*.** Entrepreneurship guarantees some amount of failure. It's a competitive endeavor. If you want to be successful as an entrepreneur, you must work hard, and that means working for many hours over a long period of time. Hard work becomes normal once you do it for a while. If you don't get how important it is to work hard, you will always be frustrated with the progress you are making. You have to hustle.

2. **Hacker:** *Be clever.* Entrepreneurship is about solving problems in novel ways that are better than the existing solutions. Once you understand the framework of business, it's time to use your creativity to bring unique solutions to the problems the world cares about. You have to have the mindset of a hacker.

3. **Hero:** *Believe in yourself.* Entrepreneurship is a mindset. When you start any entrepreneurial endeavor, you will have very little figured out. The thing that will bring about the successful execution of your endeavor is your mindset. You must believe that you can do it and know that failures are part of the process. You are your own hero.

REINVENT OR DIE

As I stated in chapter 1, the new economic mode of the world is "rapid change." The ability to reinvent yourself may start with developing a skill or becoming an entrepreneur, but in this era, you should expect that you may have to reinvent yourself several times over the course of your career.

CHAPTER THREE

* * *

SIDE HUSTLE

A CHAPTER ABOUT HOW NOT TO BURN THE BRIDGE YOU'RE STANDING ON

The leap from employee to entrepreneur is a big one. Yes, there is the mindset change that you have to make, but the skill gap you have to overcome is even bigger. To manage the risk of getting in over your head, let's walk through the process of starting a business while you're still employed.

SO YOU WANT TO BE THE BOSS

HealthStream was one of the largest internet-based companies in Nashville when I started my career there in April 2001. HealthStream had over one hundred employees on staff and went public on the NASDAQ the day before the dot-com bust. It was a great first gig for me, but I started at a difficult time for the company because of the state of the stock market for internet companies. I was not well-versed in company politics and made a few big missteps. The biggest of those was telling the CEO, Bobby Frist, that my managers were making terrible technology decisions. Not smart.

Of course the word got back to my managers and they realized they couldn't trust me, so our relationship started to deteriorate. I lasted at HealthStream for a year, and before they had a chance to fire me, I moved to a small marketing agency called Anode in 2002. I defected with one of my friends and coworkers, Scott, who was my partner in crime in falling afoul of company politics. Anode was a much better fit for me. I had a lot of autonomy and got to learn many technologies, which improved my skills. It was there that I started to get confident in my skills, as did Scott. In June 2003, we schemed up leaving Anode to start our own small firm called Skysaber. The only problem was neither one of us knew anything about how to run a company.

We each got a couple of contract gigs lined up, and with very little financial cushion, we turned in our two-week notices. I was the CEO, and I made an incredible number of mistakes. We had no sales pipeline for business. I didn't know how to build awareness for us. We didn't have solid financial models. I didn't know what we were doing, and I had no business leading a company. To be honest, I wasn't even good enough as a programmer to go out on my own yet, and that ended up being half the problem.

The beginning of the end of Skysaber, just four months after launching, was a contract I got with a one-year-old email marketing company called Emma. The contract ate up all my time, and I could not run Skysaber while under this contract. Scott called me out as a poor leader for the company, and we ended up disbanding. I was embarrassed by the failure, but also relieved to no longer be responsible as the CEO. I wasn't yet prepared to be a leader of a business. Luckily, I got along very well with the small team at Emma, and within thirty days, I became a full-time employee of the company.

When I started at Emma, our team was tiny and under a lot of stress. The co-founders of the company, Clint Smith and Will Weaver, marketed and sold the promise of the software well. However, the software wasn't working well, and customers were growing dissatisfied as they struggled to get their email campaigns out the door. I was in my first ninety days on the job, and the company was already having its "make or break" moment. The pressure was on me and the other programmer on staff, Jackson, to make the software live up to the promise of its marketing.

After weeks of trying to patch the holes in the system, Jackson and I concluded that we had to rewrite the software from scratch. This was a scary proposition for the entire team, but everyone understood this was the only option, so we forged ahead with a complete rewrite. I wasn't the best programmer in the world, but I was one of the hardest working programmers out there.

During the rewrite, there were times when we worked for two days in a row without sleep because that's what was required of us. The stress from the never-ending days of code and the fragile state of the company created a significant rift between the founders and Jackson. On the day we launched the new version of the software, Clint and Will let Jackson go.

Note: This worked out fine for Jackson. He and his father became franchisors of Plato's Closets resell clothing stores across Middle Tennessee. Today Jackson is leading this successful enterprise and a great software company he created to optimize sales in retail stores.

Somehow, through the stress, I maintained my relationship with Clint and Will. I became the default leader of technology at the company, and I held that position for the next three and a half years. As a reward for my commitment to the company, they granted me a very respectable percent of ownership in Emma. They promoted me to the title of "Director of Technology," and gave me the opportunity to grow as a manager and a leader at a company where I was almost treated like a founder. My time at Emma was one of the most transformative professional times in my life, without a doubt.

In 2006, after working at Emma for three years, I began to get an itch. When I was hired, there were six of us; now there were forty. We went from not knowing if we would make payroll to billing out $1M in a single month. I used to write software every day and now we were a team of five programmers, and I was the worst programmer on the team. My job became supporting my team and thinking about how the system could work better. I was reaching for things to get my hands dirty with and sometimes creating problems where there were none. I was getting bored.

One day I asked Will, who was my direct superior, out to lunch. At lunch, I told him I wanted to move on. I didn't know what I wanted to do yet, but I knew I wanted to do something. Will listened, didn't get mad, and asked me to hang in there because the timing wasn't right for me to move on. He was right, both for Emma and for me. Had I left Emma at that time, there would have been serious organizational issues within my team that would have been unresolved.

There were technology challenges that I had not set the team up to be successful with. For example, our database kept failing and bringing down the entire system with it, and we hadn't yet figured out why. Leaving would have been repeating the same mistake I made when I left Anode. I had no idea what I would do next; I just knew I was itching to try something new where I would be the boss.

Will, Clint, and I sat down the next day and put together a plan. We needed to bring in a senior technology leader who could bridge the gaps we had in organizational maturity and address our technology challenges. We recruited this person, Jason, and he began right away, helping us identify issues in our systems, many of which I had caused. He handled the process gracefully and gave me confidence that he would be able to, alongside our software leader, Kim, take Emma into the next era without me.

To get myself back in the game of writing code and exploring what I could do outside of Emma, I started working on a part-time contract. It was with a local electrical engineering firm that was building an RFID tracking system for a Whirlpool refrigerator plant. My old business partner, Scott, hooked me up with the opportunity.

On nights, early mornings, and weekends, I was programming again. Instead of sending emails for Emma, I was helping a manufacturing plant make sure all of its refrigerators got on the right trucks each day with all the necessary quality checks in place. It was a step towards a new small business, but I didn't quit Emma to do it. I did, however, work eighty hours a week between my role at Emma and this side hustle. During this time, it felt like only one of my Four Burners was on—the "work" one.

I set up a limited liability company (LLC) to manage this side hustle. That move gave me confidence that I wasn't just signing up for another three years at Emma. I was taking action and working toward my goal of leaving Emma and doing my own thing. My side hustle enabled me to learn how to run a business while still being a committed employee to a company that I loved.

In January 2007, I asked Will and Clint to send my coworker Jairo and I to South by Southwest (SXSW) Interactive in Austin, Texas to learn and network. This trip would provide the inspiration I needed to see the brave new world that was developing in the technology sector. SXSW deserves credit for much of my success today as a technologist who has remained ahead of the curve.

The moment at SXSW in 2007 when everything changed for me was the launch of Twitter. While Twitter had officially launched nine months prior to SXSW 2007, it was this event that put the network in the hands of tech's most influential people. I was there to experience it and get one of those early Twitter accounts.

Another important thing that happened for me in Austin

was an event I attended that happened at the same time as SXSW, but was not sanctioned by SXSW, called BarCamp Austin. BarCamp Austin was an "unconference," meaning it was free to attend and open to anyone who wanted to present to the crowd about something technology-related.

It was at BarCamp Austin, not SXSW, where I got to meet incredible entrepreneurs like Matt Mullenweg, the creator of WordPress. Spending time with ambitious creators like Matt was a game changer for me. I learned there that my internet heroes were regular people who passionately held a vision and worked hard at it. Today their products are being used by billions of people around the world.

I came back from SXSW in March with clear direction. I needed to create technology products as an entrepreneur like the people I met, and I wanted Nashville to have the same vibe that I experienced in Austin. Having built a team at Emma that could take over, I worked an extra thirty hours a week to learn what it would take to run my own ship. I'd been inspired with the direction I wanted to move in, and I knew it was time to put in my notice.

I asked Clint to go for a walk with me, and as I broke the news to him, we laughed about what a great run we'd had and agreed that the time had come for the company and me to part ways. This time I was giving three months' notice. As a bonus, Emma would sponsor and help me and my friend and fellow Emma teammate, Dave Delaney launch the first-ever BarCamp Nashville unconference. BarCamp Nashville was an incredible success, and the best launch party a new entrepreneur could ask for.

There are few things in my life that I am as proud of as the way I left Emma. It started with a respectful conversation one year in advance of my departure, developed with the determination to build a side hustle while not dropping my responsibilities at my day job, and was completed with the patience to let the inspiration for what to do next come to me.

The business I left Emma to start was a technology consultancy called Remarkable Wit. I ran it for two years, grew it to ten employees, and achieved $1 million in revenue a year before folding it into another venture. I'll tell you about Remarkable Wit in chapter 4.

THE SIDE HUSTLE IS RISK-PROOF BUT NOT LAZY-PROOF

My favorite thing about a side hustle is that it takes the biggest excuse employed people have about launching a business off the table. The infamous "I can't quit my job because I need to keep paying my bills" excuse. No one can argue that the risk of not being able to pay rent is a good reason not to leave your job to start a business. When you start a side hustle, you don't have to take on too much risk, you just have to work twice as hard.

LIMIT THE RISK WHEN YOU GO FROM SIDE HUSTLE TO FULL-ON HUSTLE

Entrepreneurship is a risky endeavor. The potential of failure is always there. We all have a responsibility to provide food, clothing, and shelter, at least to ourselves. Some of us have to do that for an entire family. The side hustle is a great way to build a bridge to your new life as an entrepreneur with limited risk. For the vast majority of us, we won't raise venture capital or take out a loan to pay for our living expenses while our business is being built. Most of us will do what's called "bootstrapping," which means launching and sustaining a business with your own resources. When you feel like it's time to quit your job, here are some practical guardrails to help you manage your risk and determine your readiness for the full-on hustle:

- **Spend less.** Work to get your personal expenses as low as possible. Learn to eat in, "Netflix and chill," and take better care of your clothes. Nothing extends the time you have on a limited income like limiting your expenses.
- **Have a cushion.** Put a minimum of three months' worth of expenses in the bank, aside from your regular spending account. That means you should have savings

to cover at least four months' expenses before you make the leap.

· **Know what's coming up.** Understand the commitments coming down the line in the next twelve to twenty-four months. Do you have any upcoming expenses that will spike your required income needs? Things like school payments for children or graduated payments for a mortgage are budget items that you can predict. Make sure you are ready for them.

THE BENEFITS OF A SIDE HUSTLE

There are major benefits that come with having a side hustle; you'll find yourself developing the very skills that will make you a better entrepreneur when you eventually take the full-time plunge.

EFFORT CAPACITY

Starting a business takes sustained effort over long periods of time. As an employee, you may think you work hard, but the scope of your efforts is limited to your position. As an entrepreneur, there is no limit to your scope. Everything is your responsibility. The only way to cover that greater scope is to spend more time working. There is no easy button. For some people, this is where they quit. They don't have the stamina to put in the hours necessary to get the business to a stable place.

When you start a business on the side, and you commit to not allowing your day job responsibilities to be neglected, you develop a greater *effort capacity*. This is a real thing that you can work on, and it's different from work ethic. This is about the patterns of work and sleep that you put your body through. Side hustles will add another twenty to thirty hours a week to your working-time budget, which pays great dividends when you go all-in on your entrepreneurial dream.

CONTEXT SWITCHING

In chapters 5 and 6, we will go in-depth on the diverse set of skills an entrepreneur must develop to be successful. But for now, let's just say as an entrepreneur, you need the ability to work on ALL parts of your business, not just the ones you like. Context switching is a term from computer science used to describe a computer storing the state of a process so it can switch from one task to another and return to the original task. It is inefficient, but it's also unavoidable as computers are required to do many different tasks within the same small window of time. And so, computer scientists develop computers to be good at context switching.

Entrepreneurs have to develop this same ability because while switching from one task to another at the drop of a dime is not ideal, a business is a dynamic, ever-changing entity, and it's necessary for the leader of a business to be able to respond to changing priorities quickly. When you have a side hustle, you are taking your brain in and out of contexts every day. One state of mind is an employee state of mind, where you need to get your work done for the company, and the other is where you need to run your enterprise on the side. This is hard, but you are developing a trait vital to your future as an entrepreneur.

BECOMING A BETTER EMPLOYEE

Okay, I know this might not make sense on the surface, but hear me out. Yes, your goal is to become an entrepreneur, which means you will be your own boss. Part of the allure and attraction of entrepreneurship is the independence it brings with it. But if you are successful as an entrepreneur, you will have employees of your own one day. The health of the relationship between a boss and their employees is not only critical to the success of a business, but to the essence of what a business stands for. The way a boss and their employees treat each other is felt throughout the company, even by the company's customers.

Much of what I learned about how to be a good boss came through becoming a good employee. I wasn't always a good employee. As I mentioned, my behavior at HealthStream left a lot to be desired, and that was reflected when I set out to launch my first company, Skysaber. My principles were all out of whack, and I was a terrible boss. At Health-

Stream, I didn't have empathy for what my boss was going through. I didn't think about what my actions were doing to my boss's peace of mind. Those shortcomings meant I would lack those same skills as a boss, when much more was on the line.

I didn't always have bosses as cool as Will and Clint, and you may not either, so I'm not suggesting you should respect people who don't respect you. But if you are fortunate to have good bosses, creating a side hustle should give you a greater appreciation for them and all the challenges they are facing. You can live up to your end of the bargain as an employee at your day job better, and these good habits will follow you into your own ventures.

As you become an entrepreneur and become your own boss, you'll find that you still have to put in real work every day. You don't leave the employee in you behind. That part of you will have to come to work every day to get things done, just like the boss in you will need to make appearances to make key leadership decisions regarding the business. You never want to lose the ability to be a great employee as you transition to entrepreneurship. It will be more valuable than you think.

DON'T BURN THAT BRIDGE

Some things are eternal truths. Do unto others as you would

have them do unto you. The world is smaller than you think. As an entrepreneur, it only gets smaller as you strive to do bigger things. If you have a great relationship with your current employer, and your side hustle outgrows your day job, treat them as you would like to be treated if you were in their shoes. When it's time to move on, be considerate. Both for your own conscience and for the potential partnerships you can have with them in the future.

CHAPTER FOUR

• • •

HOW TO GET SHIT DONE

A CHAPTER ABOUT PRODUCTIVITY

There is no traction without action. You can't think and dream your way to a successful business. You have to put numbers on the board. Learning how to be productive is critical to any entrepreneur, and that's not always as easy as it sounds.

HARD TIMES

In September 2007, I was 100 percent self-employed, running Remarkable Wit (RW). I was my company's only employee. The service RW offered was helping startups build and launch software. I signed my first customer, set my home office up, and was making good progress. Thirty days passed, and I noticed that my wife was acting distant.

Remember what I said in chapter 3 about my side hustle and running on one burner?

While taking care of my family was the reason that I worked so hard, my ambition drove me to turn my "family" burner way down. After seven years of reinvention and becoming a successful technology leader, I woke up one day to find that my wife no longer wanted to be married to me. Somewhere along the line, I missed the signs that the end was coming. I know among the many reasons we broke up was that I turned my family burner down in favor of my work burner. There are real trade-offs to that decision.

By November 2007, my wife and I separated. This wouldn't have been as bad if we didn't have children together, but we did. They were ten and eight at the time. One day shortly after the separation, I picked my eight-year-old up from school early because he was acting out in class. I knew exactly why. On the way home, I gave him space to talk about it, and he cried out, asking why we had to break up. I pulled the car onto the shoulder of the highway, got out, and held him for fifteen minutes. These were hard times.

Having made the leap into entrepreneurship and barreling into a divorce, my life was three times as complicated as it was before, and I was an emotional wreck and unable to manage it. This carried consequences.

RW won a project management contract in Sonoma County, California for a complicated piece of software. A friend who I met at HealthStream referred me for the gig. My job was to manage a developer I didn't know well, writing software with a technology that wasn't mature to create a platform no one else had ever produced. I should have spoken up in the beginning and highlighted all the challenges and the low likelihood of success with the team assembled, including myself. But it was early in my new business and I needed the work, especially since I was about to start paying alimony and child support.

Months would go by and I was paying the project about half as much attention as I needed to. The developer was way off his schedule, and it was my fault. I put the client in a precarious position. The client gave me many chances to correct the issue because they understood that I was going through a major life event. But it wasn't their problem, it was mine. The client fired me in February 2008. They should have fired me before then.

I let my client down and hurt their business because I couldn't manage my time. That failure made me consider how all aspects of my life were connected. I stopped seeing work in isolation to the rest of my life because it wasn't. If I had a big issue with my family, it would impact my ability to work. If I had too much work on my plate, it would impair my ability to take care of my health. It was all interconnected, and being effective and productive meant being intentional about time management.

HOW COULD I STAY PRODUCTIVE?

I've never been less productive than I was during the first six months of my separation from my wife. It was traumatic and the most challenging professional period of my life. What was so bad about it was that I didn't see it coming. It blindsided me and took me off my game for six months. After that, I realized that because I leaned towards being a workaholic, I needed to develop some systems to prevent (as much as possible) that from happening again.

Weird note: When my separation happened, I wasn't alone. Within a year, four male friends of mine all separated from their significant others. There was a pattern of taking the eye off the relationship for business and not realizing it had ended by the time it did.

In 2009, after two years of being single, I met a girl named Rachel. There is a different book to write about meeting your mate while suffering from the trauma of a previous relationship, but for now, I'll focus on the good parts. Rachel and I started dating from the day we met, and in 2012, I asked her to marry me. She said yes, and we set our wedding date for May 2014.

As we got closer to the wedding, we felt the intensity of the work ahead of us, and we both had plates that were piling up on us. Not having great tools to address this challenge in a romantic relationship, I leaned on the only skills I had, my fledgling business skills. I asked Rachel to spend a full day with me, planning for the next six months. Basically, I booked a business planning session for our relationship.

This planning session covered the logistics of our wedding, but it also preserved time for us to check in every month. At first, Rachel said she didn't want to "plan everything" leading up to the session, afraid that it would ruin the spontaneity that made life fun. After we finished our first one, she was thrilled that we achieved so much clarity together, and that we committed and protected time for our relationship and our new family. Since that day, we've made this planning session a tradition. Every six months, we block out an entire day to talk about what's important for us over the next six months. The output of the session is clarity on our goals and desires and committing time and resources to those things and each other.

This isn't a book about relationships. However, most people want to be in one or are in one, so let's acknowledge that your productivity is related to the health of your relationships. When there are major issues in your relationships, your productivity suffers. These planning sessions with my wife are key to my productivity. They give me peace of mind that I haven't forgotten about my family burner.

THE TIME BUDGET

A skill I've developed as an entrepreneur, reflected in my biannual planning session ritual, is my commitment to *take time to manage my time*. I see the act of working on my calendar to design the way I spend time as key to maintaining control over the ever-growing demands for my time. As you build a business, how you spend your time becomes a key success factor. There are always people wanting to meet up for reasons that don't benefit you or your business. It's your responsibility to manage your time as diligently as you manage your money to ensure you are investing it wisely.

These days, managing your time is becoming increasingly difficult because of all the ways that people can easily send you a request. Email, text messages, LinkedIn, Facebook, Twitter, Instagram, and more all buzzing on your phone, which is with you all the time. These requests can come from all over the world, so there is no nine-to-five anymore when it comes to responding to people about work. The math doesn't work and you cannot allow everyone to access you whenever they want or you will never do the things you tell yourself you want to do.

To address this, I manage a time budget on my calendar that

reflects what my ideal week would look like. I reserve blocks of time for creating, meetings with my partners, my family, working out, eating, and resting. Once those blocks of time are reserved, there are only a few remaining blocks available for me to spend that don't have an assigned purpose. I always keep some blocks of time open because that leaves room for serendipity or interruptions to happen. Some of the best opportunities come when I haven't planned them. But a time budget is an essential tool for me to enforce a protocol of productivity by assigning priorities to my time.

	SUN 8	MON 9	TUE 10	WED 11	THU 12	FRI 13	SAT 14
All Day	Rest Day / Weekly Preparation Day	Brio Day / Medium Workout Day	Content and Meeting Day / Heavy Workout Day	Light Workout Day / Well-Being Day	Content and Meeting Day / Heavy Workout Day	Brio Day / Light Workout Day	Medium Workout Day
8am		Creative Time (No Meetings)	Creative Time (No Meetings)		Weekly Breakfast with Chris or LeShane		
9am				Creative Time (No Meetings)		Vic Meeting	Hyperbolic Stretching
10am	Shopping & Food Prep	Brio Working Day - Work, Meetings	Weekly Together TN Meeting or 1/2/3/4 Star Meetings		Undisputed / Creative Power Meeting	GHI Meeting	
11am				Shopping & Food Prep		Brio Work (No Meetings)	Yong In Belt Test
12am			Hyperbolic Stretching		Hyperbolic Stretching		
1pm	Writing, GTD, Finances	Running & Sauna	Strength Training		Strength Training	Pilates w/ Laurel	Strength Training
2pm			Eat	Pilates w/ Laurel	Eat	Running & Sauna	
3pm		H:F Content (Writing/Recordings) or Brio Meetings	MW Content Recording		MW Content Recording or Creative Time	Brio Work: Email, Asana, Productive Work PRIORITY. To Be Booked	
4pm		Eat	Eat	Eat	Eat	Eat	
5pm		JSF Office Hours			One or Two Star Calls		
	Meditation at Home	Meditation at Home	Meditation at Home	Meditation at Home	Meditation at Home	Meditation at Home	Meditation at Home
6pm		Snack	Snack	Snack	Snack	Snack	
7pm		Travel + Competition BJJ	BJJ (Intermediate / Advanced)	Hump Day Fun or 1st Week Family Dinner (Do Not Book 1st week of Month)	BJJ (Intermediate / Advanced)	Date Night	
8pm	Sunday Family Dinner	Dinner					
9pm			Hapkido		Hapkido		
10pm							

THE VIRTUAL ASSISTANT

It's difficult for me to tell someone who wants to meet for coffee that I'm not available for three months, which sometimes happens. I never want to seem like I'm better than others or upset someone hoping to meet with me, but getting things done requires being strict with the access others have to your calendar. Having a virtual assistant who handles my scheduling and takes care of the dirty work of forcing people to work within my constraints is a gift that I gave myself when my business could afford to pay for it.

Virtual assistants now come in many flavors, everything from overseas call centers to artificial intelligence software. If your time is in such demand that you have to push people out a month or more to meet with you, you can afford a virtual assistant. I was skeptical of the value of a virtual assistant for years, but now that I work with one, I can't imagine not having her on the team.

BEWARE THE BRAIN PICKERS

It's important to qualify people's reasons for wanting to get on your calendar in order to protect your time from other people's demands and priorities. It can be a real ego boost to have someone say that they want to pick your brain, but it can also pull you away from the work you need to do to achieve your goals. I believe in reserving time for mentoring and advising others, but this requires real time-management or it can get out of control quickly.

You don't need to spend a full hour over coffee with someone who just wants to ask you questions they haven't even thought through. Can you give them what they need in fifteen minutes? Maybe even five? Do you need to meet them in person, or can you handle it on a phone call or through email? Sometimes you just need to turn a person down or refer them to others. If you aren't willing to say no to requests for your time, you are saying to yourself that the needs of others supersede your own. Get over this fear and start managing these requests more critically.

ACCEPTING UNPREDICTABILITY

All the planning in the world can't make up for the fact that you don't control everything happening around you. Life is not as predictable as the time budget in your calendar. There are freak incidents that throw off an entire day that you have to learn how to absorb. Some times of year are more frantic than others. A big part of being productive is based on how well you handle unpredictable scenarios, as well as how accepting you are of the requirements that different seasons of life have of you.

No matter how much you try to create structure around your day, the truth is you are not in complete control of what each day has in store for you. Make sure to allow space for small interruptions and know that a lot can change on a day-to-day basis. Using a time budget is great, but don't lose it when something occurs that you didn't expect and you have to spend time outside of what your budget prescribes. How you react to these unpredictable events impacts your energy and can cause you to be less productive overall.

STORMING AND SETTLING: ACKNOWLEDGING SEASONALITY

I've never avoided the seasonality and weather patterns of business. Some periods of the year are intense, and some aren't. Some weeks are so packed that you can't even see straight because you're just running from event to event, and some weeks your schedule is wide open. This pattern of *Storming and Settling* is a rhythm that you have to make peace with.

During the storm, you may not exercise as much as you'd like, or keep your house as clean as normal. It's just not rea-sonable...you're in the middle of a storm and things are flying around. But the storm won't last forever. There will come a time when it settles, and you'll recalibrate and recover.

One tactic that ensures you are managing your *settling time* well is reserving regular appointments to ensure that you take care of yourself. For me, that looks something like:

- Weekly cleanup of email to "Inbox Zero," usually on Sundays.
- Twice a month, review of the budget. Once high level, once deep dive.
- One weekend day a month for cleanup of all systems (I always find important things in old text messages, LinkedIn messages, Evernote, Asana. etc.).
- Committed exercise at least twice a week (for storms) and five or more times a week ideally.
- Quarterly trips away from home with Rachel, even if it's only for forty-eight hours.
- Twice-a-year planning sessions with Rachel of our calendar, budget, and goals.
- One family trip and one couple's trip a year that are at least four days.

I carry this model into the work environment by committing to regular touchpoints with my business partners and employees so that we become aligned and maintain our relationship. When we go too long without these check-ins, things fray.

The magic of these *settle times* is that they give me peace when I'm in the storm. The storm is temporary, and a moment of settling is around the corner. Knowing this allows me to relax in the storm, seeing it as a burst of progress in my journey without being overwhelmed by it.

OCCASIONALLY, YOU WILL GIVE UP SLEEP

I hate to say this because I know how valuable sleep is for your productivity, and losing sleep ultimately hurts both productivity and the quality of your work. However, I've found no way to avoid this reality. When you put ambition together with unpredictability, you will arrive at a moment where a deadline doesn't allow for eight hours of sleep.

Sleep is critical to our health and sharpness of mind, so I always advocate for getting as close to eight hours of sleep as you can. But, sometimes it's just not going to happen. Sometimes you have to pull an all-nighter to hit a deadline. It's part of the deal. Embrace it, and be sure to take time to recuperate on the other side.

HOW TO BE MOST PRODUCTIVE IN YOUR ACTUAL WORK

We've talked a lot about managing and protecting time so that the important things never get pushed too far aside. This is the first step to getting important shit done. Now let's talk about how to work most effectively in that time you've protected! Here are three principles that can help you blaze through your list of to-dos like a machine.

THE IRON TRIANGLE

One of the biggest challenges with successfully completing

a project is having a project that can be successful in the first place. My Sonoma County software project, for example, was not designed for success from the beginning. What that project taught me was that before even starting on a project, I need to assess if I can execute it. A trusty model for that assessment is "The Iron Triangle."

The Iron Triangle comprises three things: Time (deadlines), Scope (everything we are trying to get done), and Resources (usually people, but it can include other resources as well).

Whenever you undertake a project, assess it with the Iron Triangle. Any successful project must have a scope that matches the allocated resources and time. If these three things don't match, and you can't increase your resources or you can't push out your deadline, then you need to adjust your scope.

Failing to assess a project through the Iron Triangle before starting leads to being overwhelmed by the challenge of making an impossible recipe of time, resources, and scope work. This stops people from doing anything because they are wringing their hands about the impossibility of making it all fit.

Getting shit done is about project management, whether it's for professional or personal projects or even a string of small tasks. If you can't negotiate time, scope, and resources, you can't start with a clear path to your finish line. Years of software development taught me I would never create a perfect piece of software. Emma wasn't perfect, but it was good enough to become a multimillion-dollar business. We did the best we could with the time and resources we had. I've carried this thought process through in just about everything I've done since, and it's how I get things done.

THE IMPORTANCE OF BATCHING

In chapter 2, I spoke about how competency in context switching is valuable for entrepreneurs. But at its core, context switching is inefficient because it involves you performing one kind of task, and then stopping and switching to a different kind of task, only to return back to the original kind of task that will require reorientation. Context switching is sometimes necessary, but never ideal. If you want to be productive, the ideal approach is to batch your work. That means setting aside a block of time for doing the same type of task to achieve deep focus and optimal efficiency.

This seems obvious, but many people don't organize their to-do lists for batching. For example, it is more efficient to work through all of your emails, than it is to send an email, make a call, and then send another email. If you take time to categorize the different types of tasks you do and batch them together, you will save time and improve the quality of the work because you aren't context switching.

You've probably heard of Pareto's Principle as the "80/20 rule." It was named after an Italian economist named Vilfredo Pareto, who, in 1896, wrote a paper that identified 20 percent of people in Italy owned 80 percent of the land. Pareto then applied this 80/20 ratio to other phenomena such as peas in a garden. Astoundingly, 20 percent of the pea pods yielded 80 percent of the peas. Over time, Pareto's Principle has evolved to mean that 20 percent of something produces 80 percent of the value of that thing.

Let's apply the 80/20 rule to productivity: imagine that only 20 percent of our time produces 80 percent of the value. If this is true, then you have to review your time spent working and ask, "Am I doing the most value-producing tasks?" and "Do I spend at least 20 percent of my time on those value-producing activities?" If you aren't, then you have to look at yourself and determine what changes you need to make in how you assign work to yourself. Productivity without impact is useless. You always want to focus on making your productivity valuable.

TECHNOLOGY

Technology, especially internet-enabled technology, multiplies the impact of the productivity principles we just reviewed.

Time tracking, project management, communication, accounting, analytics, and low-cost labor for tasks that can be completed within twenty-four hours for $5-$100. You can achieve these things (and much more) faster with technology. Some people are romantic about how they work (taking notes using pen and paper, for example), not understanding that their business doesn't operate in a vacuum. The business world is hypercompetitive, and the companies that win are leveraging technology to work better, smarter, and faster for the benefit of their customer.

I've leaned into technology because it's the foundation of my skills in business. Consistently embracing new best-of-breed technology has been key to my success. I couldn't have achieved what I have if I hadn't spent a significant percentage of my time keeping up with the newest capabilities that technology offered. Being a practitioner, always rolling up my sleeves and learning something new has been the key to growing with tech and not being left behind. I'm certain that if you commit time and energy to leveraging technology, you can multiply your productivity.

WHAT CAN PRODUCTIVITY DO FOR YOU?

I have personally used productivity as a superpower to achieve success. I've found it to be a differentiator and a competitive advantage in the market. When you are productive, you do more with the one thing we all have the same amount of: time. This means I can be a business leader, a board member for nonprofits I care about, and a family man engaged with his wife and children.

It also means I can pay attention to my health and even fit in some time to spend with my friends. Being more productive means I can game the Four Burners Theory. It's a hack for entrepreneurs who want to live a full life.

CHAPTER FIVE

* * *

THE EIGHT CORE CONCEPTS PART I: INSIDE THE BUILDING

A CHAPTER ABOUT THE FOUNDATION OF BUSINESS

All complex organisms are governed by simple principles. Businesses are no different. If you don't understand the fundamentals, you will always have blind spots and spend energy in unwise ways. There is an order to the inner workings of a business, a natural order. The next two chapters are dedicated to teaching you this order.

You must maintain balance of what's happening outside your "building" versus what's happening inside your "building." I use *building* as a metaphor for the separation between how businesses operate internally versus the way they work in the market.

Inside your building is your process, your culture, your team, and what they think about you.

Outside your building is your customer, how you engage with them, and what they think about you.

At Remarkable Wit, I was way too focused on what was happening outside my building, and not focused enough on what was happening inside the building. This is common, and most entrepreneurs can't cover both well at the same time. It's all too common for entrepreneurs to focus too much on either the inside or outside of the building. This leads to an imbalance that can topple a business before long.

Through the RW experience and other businesses I've been involved in, I've come to understand that businesses are complex systems made up of interdependent, distinct concepts. These concepts must be understood, prioritized, and balanced in order for the overall system to work.

As a software architect, one of the most important skills to develop is organizing ideas into concepts that could be implemented as code. We call this *creating frameworks*. When I realized I would be an entrepreneur for the rest of my career, I started seeking a framework I could use to build and grow businesses. I didn't find one. In fact, many business people I talked to about business frameworks insisted that every business was different and coming up with a framework was foolish.

After more than a decade as a practitioner of entrepreneurship and five years as a venture capitalist with over eighty portfolio companies, I've codified a framework we can view all businesses through. I call this framework the **Eight Core Concepts**.

Every business is built upon Eight Core Concepts that are intimately related to each other. These Eight Core Concepts are connected by a model of dependency and inheritance. Many successful entrepreneurs operate through these core concepts, but wouldn't be able to articulate their model. My hope is that the framework of the Eight Core Concepts is a novel and helpful tool to both the neophyte and the well-traveled entrepreneur.

I organize the concepts into two groups: external and internal. This follows the 'outside the building' versus 'inside the building' metaphor that I described earlier. I have prioritized them from most vital to least vital. This is an inevitable point of debate, but here we go:

The Eight Core Concepts are:

- Internal
  - Leadership
  - Finance
  - Operations
  - Growth
- External
  - Product
  - Service
  - Sales
  - Marketing

Each concept serves a distinct purpose which can be distilled to one sentence:

- The main purpose of leadership is to create a **culture in which a business can thrive.**
- The main purpose of finance is to ensure **sustainability of the business.**
- The main purpose of operations is to minimize **risk of the business.**
- The main purpose of growth is **optimization of the business.**
- The main purpose of product is to produce **a predictable unit of value.**
- The main purpose of service is to **maximize customer satisfaction.**
- The main purpose of sales is to **generate revenue.**
- The main purpose of marketing is to **identify, understand, and generate demand.**

All of these concepts are critical to business, but the order in which I listed them is intentional. **Leadership is the most important part of any business.** Every other concept both depends on it and inherits from it. As you move out from leadership, the same is true of every concept after it. Finance depends on and inherits from leadership, but is core to all the other core concepts of a business. Operations depends on and inherits from finance, and so on.

What's counterintuitive about this framework is that if you get hung up on the "priority," you'll miss the importance of inheritance. In computer science, inheritance means that an object has all the capabilities of the object it inherits from, plus its own new capabilities. If you apply this to the Eight Core Concepts framework, it means that while marketing is the least core of the eight concepts, it is the most comprehensive. Marketing has aspects of leadership, finance, operations, growth, product, service, and sales within it. It is the only concept comprehensive of all other business concepts, and that's why marketers are so elevated in today's business world.

> Note: Marketing is my favorite of all the concepts.

I designed this framework for understanding businesses to make it clear that even though you are gifted in a particular area, you have to develop a basic understanding of all these concepts to be an effective business leader. It also orients you around leadership, which is the only job that you cannot delegate.

There are many business books that will do a better job than this one at detailing each of these concepts. The purpose of presenting the eight core concepts framework is to:

- ensure the concepts are memorable,
- establish the hierarchy of importance of the concepts,
- define the special relationships between the concepts that result from inheritance,
- structure the nature of the concepts as internal vs. external.

I will now summarize each concept and point you toward other great books that tackle these topics in depth. Let's start inside the building.

LEADERSHIP

Whether planning to build a company with one hundred employees or just a great lifestyle business for yourself, leadership is a capability that you have to develop. In entrepreneurship, leadership is being responsible for one's ownership of the business. Leaders respond to challenges that come up as a business develops, and challenges never cease.

The primary purpose of leadership is **creating a culture in**

which a business can thrive. Not every culture can enable a business to thrive. In fact, most businesses do not have cultures that enable them to thrive, and that's why most businesses fail. When people list the reasons why their business failed, they often point to things further down the core concept list. "The product wasn't good enough" or "the sales team sucked." That's a sign that the culture isn't optimal for business and that there is a lack of accountability.

Entrepreneurs blame failure on a lack of product-market fit, a poor sales team, a lack of finances, etc. But these problems are derivatives of a failure in leadership. Somewhere along the line, the culture created by the leader did not inspire the right response to the downstream challenge, and they allowed the downstream challenge to tank the business. Most successful business people have lived through a moment where their company was on the threshold of dying, but a bold response saved the day. No one gets through unscathed. Strong leadership is always a requisite for success.

VISION AND VALUES

Leadership is responsible for the two most important aspects that make a company unique: its vision statement and values. I use vision statement as an all-encompassing word for what drives a company forward. Many books have been written on vision and values, and there is debate about how leaders should craft them. Some say a company should be anchored in its purpose or its "why." Others say the mission is the way to orient the company because it can be measurable, it ties to a goal, and is more prescriptive than subjective. It's up to you, the leader, to decide what model works best for you. Whatever model you choose, there must be a vision (or purpose, or mission, or why, etc.) there, and it must be omnipresent.

There are several books that give good models on how to develop vision and values for your organization. For early stage entrepreneurs, *Traction* by Gino Wickman is one of the best I have read. It offers a clear structure and format for entrepreneurs to follow in crafting a vision and values as an organizational infrastructure. Simon Sinek's *Start with Why* is also great for distilling the purpose of your company to a *why* statement.

It's not worth spending time to come up with your own model to craft a vision statement or values. Your energy is better spent creating the vision and values themselves. What's important is that you don't skip this step. Vision and values are necessary for you to create alignment with your team and determine where alignment is missing. The vision and values established by the leaders of the company become the living law of the company. They are the primary guidance for the culture of the company.

There's one piece of guidance I can provide on crafting your vision statement: the vision should be customer-centric. This brings to mind the "Jobs to Be Done" theory created by the late innovation thought leader, Clayton Christensen. The theory's premise is that a customer has a job to do, and it's a company's job to help their customer get that job done well. When creating your vision, the more you orient around helping your customer get their job done well, the more empathetic and customer-centric your organization's culture will be.

MANAGEMENT

Management is a skill set that combines art and science. The Merriam-Webster definition of management is:

> "the act or art of managing: the conducting or supervising of something (such as a business)."

I love this definition because it acknowledges that managing is an art, which in my experience, is 100 percent the truth. There is no one way to managing things because the approach will reflect the values of the person who is doing the management. I also love the use of the word "conducting," which implies orchestration. So far, we've talked a lot about the Creative Power that we are trying to access via entrepreneurship. But I haven't brought up orchestration until now. I'll dig into this in more detail in chapter 12: Orchestrate. But who leads an orchestra? The conductor.

The Merriam-Webster definition of conducting is:

1. to direct or take part in the operation or management of
2. to direct the performance of
3. to lead from a position of command.

Management is the art AND science of leading an operation. Operations require management of people, projects, process, quality, change, boards, and on and on. Management is a key aspect of leadership that cannot be overlooked. As the leader, you must have management capabilities and always work on developing them. Even if you are a one-person company, you have to manage yourself.

Management is where leaders hold the organization (and themselves) accountable to the vision and values of the organization. This accountability covers all commitments that the organization has made to its owners, employees, partners, and customers. The quality of management that exists in any organization will have a direct impact on the success of the company.

There are many competing schools of thought on management, so it's difficult to recommend any one to you. Peter Drucker is often referred to as the "father of management thinking," and his works (especially his essential book on the topic titled *Management*) are likely useful to review. I encourage you to explore as many as you like until you find one that resonates with you.

ENTREPRENEURSHIP DEPENDS ON LEADERSHIP

Leadership is the most important concept in a business, period. It's what you must do, and cannot delegate at any time. The most important aspect of creation in a business is its vision and values. If copied from another business, you might as well work for that business. Vision and values are where you call on your Creative Power and make your mark on the world. Everything aligns to your vision and values, and they must be infused into all aspects of the business through effective management. This is the most difficult thing in the business world to do, but if done well, will give you the foundation to build a successful company.

FINANCE

It seems self-explanatory that a business needs to have a handle on its finances. Yet most new entrepreneurs don't understand the importance of finance in their business. In my experience, finance is the aspect of business that most new entrepreneurs are weakest in. Understanding finance is critical to ensuring the **sustainability of your business.**

I didn't enter entrepreneurship with a great mind for finance. I knew I had developed into a functional entrepreneur when I could manage the day-to-day finances of my business without driving my company into the ground. That meant all the bills got paid, we collected money from those who owed us, and I knew whether we were OK on cash flow or about to hit a cash crunch.

There are six key finance terms you have to know:

1. *Revenue* is the money a company receives from its customers for the value it delivers to them.
2. *Expenses* are costs the company incurs in doing business.
3. *Profit* (sometimes called earnings) is the money the company keeps from the revenue received after paying all of its expenses.
4. *Assets* are the items and resources owned by the company that determine its value.
5. *Liabilities* are debt and other financial obligations that a company has that count against its value.
6. *Capital* is money that comes into your business as an investment or a loan, or money that your company uses to invest or to loan money to others. It's not the same as revenue since it's not earned. When capital refers to an investment, it adds to the value of the company. This changes the ownership structure as capital is invested in exchange for ownership in the company.

Once you understand these six key terms, you can have 80 percent of the conversations you need to have about the financial health of your company.

There are four key aspects of finance that an entrepreneur needs to understand to be competent:

- Accounting
- Day-to-day finance management
- Budgeting and modeling
- The balance sheet

ACCOUNTING

If you've ever wondered if you need a Certified Public Accountant (CPA) for your business, the answer is yes. No business can properly function without a CPA for two reasons.

First, you need to build what's called a Chart of Accounts to categorize how money flows in (*revenue*) and out (*expenses*) of your business. You could build your own chart of accounts, but it will probably be wrong because there is, in fact, a *right way* to design a chart of accounts.

The right way is called Generally Accepted Accounting Principles or GAAP for short, and unless you are a CPA or studying to become one, you probably don't know GAAP.

Also, it's not key to the success of your business that you know GAAP. What is important is that your business runs as close to GAAP compliance as possible. This will make your ability to switch accounting software, finance personnel, and accounting firms much easier. If your business grows, you will switch one or more of those things at some point.

Second, you need an accountant for taxes. The rules for filing your taxes each year are mind-numbing, constantly changing, and just a little different for each business. Every business operates differently, and that impacts how their taxes are filed. Yes, you can handle your accounting yourself with software. However the time you spend trying to figure out how to file your taxes each year is not worth the money you will save. You should find a firm who can expertly handle this for you, period.

DAY-TO-DAY FINANCE MANAGEMENT

Managing the day-to-day finances of your business is the one area that I recommend every entrepreneur do at first because it will teach you how your business runs. The good news is that there are plenty of wonderful software tools out there that can help you manage your day-to-day finances with relative ease. No tool does the work for you, but they do empower a novice person who works hard to get the job done by themselves.

A note on tools: I don't endorse any tools, but you've no

doubt heard of QuickBooks. There are many alternatives to QuickBooks today that provide different flavors of the same capabilities. I use a company called Bench instead of QuickBooks for my day-to-day finance needs because it's not just software. It's a team of bookkeepers who interact with you through software for a fixed monthly fee. I have other tools that I use for special aspects of finance. Gusto, for example, is my go-to tool for small business payroll.

Your day-to-day finance management will cover the following areas:

- Cash flow management
- Payroll
- Accounts Payable (AP) and Accounts Receivable (AR)
- The income statement (also known as the profit-and-loss statement)

Cash flow management means you ensure that you have enough money in the bank to operate the business. You should have a data-driven understanding of when money is coming in and out of the business. You should be able to look into the future and predict where you may run out of money and create a plan to prevent it. This is the most basic aspect of finance, and you probably have some method of doing this in your personal life. The difference in business is there are more expenses related to upkeep than in your personal life.

Payroll is the process of paying your employees in a way that is compliant with federal and state laws. It's a complex matter and you shouldn't handle it alone. Fortunately, there are many services and software tools that can make this process very easy to manage. Consult your accountant, but also understand your working style and make sure your accountant understands your working style before selecting a payroll service.

I've found that accountants like to force their clients into the tools that best suit them. But if you have to use the tool, it's important that you are comfortable with the tool. Regardless, the payroll service tool that you select should take care of the complexity of managing payroll. You should just be responsible for making sure there is enough money in the bank and that raises, bonuses, and commissions are properly entered into the system.

Accounts receivable (AR) is how you track what customers owe your business. Accounts payable (AP) is what you owe creditors, vendors, suppliers, and utilities. AR and AP are how you track revenue and expenses in your business. Unless your business collects cash up-front or on a subscription where you have a credit card on file, expect that your customers will not pay you on time. You have to follow up with them to receive payment. This process is called collections, and I'm sure you've heard of it. Accounts receivable is an *asset*, because it represents future value (money expected to be collected) in your business.

Accounts payable, the money you owe others, is a *liability*. Remember I said half of your invoices won't be paid on time? Well, managing accounts payable is why. Manage your outgoing cash flow in a way that benefits you. Don't send out money based on everyone else's due dates. Batch payments to others on regular dates each month, for example, twice a month.

If money is tight, choose which bills get paid and which ones you will allow to go into collections. This isn't ideal. You should strive to pay all your bills on time, but don't let anyone tell you that everyone doesn't do this. Some of my biggest collections' issues have come from very large corporations who have plenty of money to pay, but only pay when it is advantageous to them.

This tug of war between AR and AP can have a significant impact on cash flow. You need to have your hand on the pulse of cash flow until you can hire a head of finance to manage this better than you can. Even then, you must understand it enough to ask your head of finance the right questions. You can never abdicate the responsibility of asking the right questions to those who work for you. That's part of leadership, always being accountable.

Finally, we have the *income statement*, also known as the

profit-and-loss statement. This is the snapshot of your business's revenue (money in, not including investments or loans) and expenses (money out) in a particular period of time. An income statement will be created for a monthly, quarterly, or annual view to determine if the business is profitable or not. The categories of revenue and expenses found in the income statement will come from the chart of accounts that your accountant has designed for you.

The income statement tells you whether you were in the red (lost money) or the black (made a profit) in a particular period of time. This statement answers the question: "Is your business profitable?" It also can tell you how much money you are losing. As you can see, this is an important finance report, and as an entrepreneur, you have to master it.

BUDGETING AND MODELING

You've probably heard the term *business model*. In simple terms, your business model is: Who your customers are, what your value is to them, why that value is unique, and how you deliver that value to them. Once you've defined your business model, you must support that business model with a financial model. Your financial model is made up of the numbers you use to make your business model work, and it shows that the business will (eventually) be profitable. Every business in the world, no matter how simple or complex, has to be financially modeled, otherwise it has no foundation for functioning.

A financial model will use your chart of accounts and looks very similar to your income statement. It starts with two simple categories—revenue and expenses. Revenue goes on top, expenses go below. What comes out of the bottom is the profit or loss that the business results produce. The model will take critical assumptions about your revenue and expenses and will give you a view of how the business will work. Assumptions like how many customers you'll have, how much revenue you'll generate per customer, and how much it will cost to deliver value to each customer. In order for a business model to work, your assumptions need to result in a profitable result at the bottom of the model.

Creating a financial model is a discovery exercise, where you, as the entrepreneur, develop an in-depth understanding of your business. The more experienced you become at running businesses, the better you will become at financial modeling. That's because experience will help you identify three modeling traps you should always look for to offset your irrational optimism and desire to make the business work on paper:

1. You are often overconfident about the amount of revenue you will generate.
2. You are often missing critical expenses to operate your business.

3. You are often understating your expenses.

You have to address these three financial modeling traps proactively. You should build your model, and then step outside of yourself with your confidence and optimism, and do an audit of your financial model, looking for these three lies. Doing this will bring your model much closer to reality, giving your company a better chance of success.

Modeling is what you do when you are designing your business. Budgeting is what you do once your model is "complete" and it's time to commit to numbers that your company will deliver. I put *complete* in quotes because every experienced entrepreneur knows that a financial model is a living document and it is never truly complete. It evolves as you learn more about the realities of your business and as the market changes. Vendors will charge you more, employees will demand raises, and customers will leave you. These things impact your business and have to be accounted for in your financial model. Even with the understanding that your model will evolve over time, you have to choose a version of the model to create a budget from that the company will commit to achieving.

Meeting your budgets in business requires more discipline than meeting your personal budget. Most of us evolve our personal budgets quarterly if not monthly, even though we shouldn't. In business, you must lock a budget in by the beginning of the fiscal year. Your fiscal year is the beginning and end of your business's budgeted year. Most businesses should match their fiscal year to the calendar year, but sometimes a business's fiscal year will run from July to June, or some other non-calendar year format.

As you enter your fiscal year and start having real results, you will report what's happening against what you budgeted for. In finance terms, these reported results are called "actuals," and these numbers show up in a report called "budget vs. actual," which combines your income statement (actuals) and your budget. This report will allow you to track how you are performing against what you thought would happen at the beginning of the year.

THE BALANCE SHEET

Once your business is up and running, you will do day-to-day finance management. On a monthly, quarterly, and annual basis, you'll compare your results against your budget to track your performance. While that is happening, there is another financial tale developing about your business. That story is told on your balance sheet.

The balance sheet is the report that covers the assets, liabilities, and capital in the business. This report gives you a view of the value of the company. The balance sheet is a key document used to determine the value of a company for a transaction like a merger or an acquisition. It's also used in not-so-great situations like bankruptcy or liquidation. The balance sheet shows the undisputed base value of the company and will be used in the valuation process when seeking capital from banks, private markets, or in acquisition negotiations.

Let's take a minute to discuss determining a value for a company that is being acquired. Depending on the market that your company is in and the type of company you have, the actual valuation process will vary. For example, companies that provide a service without a technology component, like a marketing agency, are usually valued at a modest multiple of the last year's revenue. This could be one-and-one-half to three times the revenue generated in the previous year. If the agency is doing really well, they could justify being valued on their projected earnings and/or at a larger multiple.

If you are running a software-as-a-service (SAAS) company, the multiple could be much higher, maybe seven to ten times the revenue. And it could be a multiple of the following year's projected revenue, not the current one. The business model of an SAAS company scales better than a pure service company and is less dependent on the team operating the business. Because it scales better, it demands a premium multiple on its value.

If you are shutting a company down, the balance sheet will be the key tool in extracting value. You will start by paying off the liabilities of the company and then selling off the assets to generate a return for the shareholders.

Businesses live and die by their finances, and most entrepreneurs do not understand enough about how finances work, so they don't understand how their own business works. After leadership, finances are the most important aspect of building a business. The detail I just provided gives you 20 percent of the information you need to handle 80 percent of the finance situations you will encounter in your business.

OPERATIONS

Once you get beyond finance, you can then move to how the business functions on a daily, weekly, monthly, quarterly, and yearly basis. This concept of *how* a business functions is called operations. Operations comes after finance because it has a simple purpose—to ensure the budget is met. Operations serves to make the financial model work.

When you start a business, everything is procedural. There are steps to getting up and running. You need to have a name for the business. You need a business license and articles of incorporation for the state that you are operating in. You need a bank account, and on and on. There is a critical list of items you need to secure just to legally operate the business, but this is not the only critical list you need in the business. You need a critical list of things that must be executed for your business to function. This leads to the reason operations falls right after finances in the Eight Core Concepts. At its core, the purpose of operations is the indefatigable **elimination of risk** in the business.

If an accountant is the key expert on finances for an entrepreneur, then an attorney is the key expert on operations for an entrepreneur. Risk comes in many forms, but the most dangerous ones come in an instant and can wipe out the company. Most entrepreneurs wait too long to prepare for these risks. They should be addressed as soon as possible. It's the entrepreneur's job to assess the risks in every situation and come up with the right solution for each scenario. There are present risks versus future risks that often have to be weighed, and these decisions are constantly being presented.

THE FORM OF THE COMPANY

When you operate a business, you do so under the laws of the city and/or county, state and/or territory and country in which your business is based. As soon as you set up a business, you are at risk of running afoul of those jurisdictions. Your attorney should ensure that your paperwork is correct and that you are choosing the right form of business to limit the amount of risk to you personally.

The form of company you choose impacts how you file taxes and the level of liability that you personally assume for the actions of the company. For example, operating as a sole proprietor means that you, the individual, are liable for all claims against the business without exception. I can't think of a situation where this is beneficial, yet many people set up their businesses as sole proprietorships. This is done because they don't have attorneys, they don't understand the risks they are taking on, and a sole proprietorship is the easiest and least expensive form of business to set up.

The most popular form of a company over the last two decades is the Limited Liability Company or LLC. An LLC is a simple form of company to set up, has a favorable taxation structure, and limits the liability of the owners from claims made against the company.

Corporations take the separation of owner and company a step further because they are different entities entirely in the eyes of the Internal Revenue Service (IRS). While a corporation may offer more liability protections than an LLC, it is not as favorable from a tax perspective. Because a corporation is a different entity from its owners, it is taxed, and then the individuals who own the company are taxed on any income they earn. This double tax issue is one of the main reasons that LLCs have become so popular in recent years. LLCs are not taxed explicitly; the profit of an LLC is passed through to the owners, and the owners are the ones who are taxed.

PROTECTING THE BUSINESS WITH INSURANCE

Once you get beyond the form of business, the next risks to tackle are the threats to your business that are beyond your control. The only way to do this is with insurance. There are various forms of insurance that a business can have. Starting with General Liability, which protects the business from claims involving injury due to the operation of the business. From there, depending on the business that you operate, there are other more specialized types of insurance that you can get for your business to protect it.

One thing that insurance is important for is natural disasters or acts of God. If your business has property that is necessary to operate the business like computers, or requires a building like a retail store, a powerful storm could put you out of business for a long time. If you aren't properly insured, the losses incurred from such an event could be irrecoverable. A commercial insurance broker can walk you through the risks that your business has and the different policies you should consider to cover yourself.

There are too many types of insurance to cover in this book, so again, get an attorney and an insurance broker to review your business and give you guidance on where you are exposed. Where vulnerabilities exist, get them covered with the proper form of insurance.

GET IT IN INK

Remember when I said that the lawyer is the key expert for your operations department? Well here's why: You need a contract for everything you do in the company. Like to do business on a handshake? Yeah, that's nice in the movies, but in the real world, you'll need a contract. Want to hire an employee? You'll need a contract for that. Not ready for employees, but want to hire contractors? Yeah, that requires a contract too. How about a website? With privacy laws these days, you'll need a contract for the visitors of your website.

I think you get the point. Again, since different businesses need different contracts, the best thing to do is document everything your business will do that touches other people— employees, contractors, vendors, customers, potential customers, investors, partners. All these parties will need a contract from you. If you have your contracts ready on the front end, you will be efficient in dealmaking, and you will understand your business better.

Pro Tip: If your attorney is any good, they will have boilerplate versions of just about every contract you need as a starting point. You shouldn't pay your attorney to create these contracts from scratch. If your attorney says you need to have this from scratch, then ask them if this is the first one they've ever done. If it is, then that's a sign you may need help from a different attorney.

HUMAN RESOURCES

The next significant thing you need to address in the operations category is your employees. Hiring employees for your business is a massive undertaking. If you thought about all the risk you took on once you started bringing on employees, you might never hire anyone. But it's very hard to grow a business without employees, so you might as well get used to it.

Once you add employees to your business, the risks quickly move beyond compliance with the law. Now the risk expands to threats on your culture. It's easy to maintain your company culture when you are the only employee. Once you add people into your business, they will test your culture. Human Resources (HR) is a complicated aspect of operations because it deals with the most complex part of your business, the humans who work there.

HR contains the following key aspects that need to be in place before you bring your first employee on board:

Compliance

You must operate in compliance with the laws of the country, state and city/county in which you live. That means you have to know those laws and have processes and documents in place to keep your company compliant. You can outsource this to a third-party vendor like a payroll company or a professional employer organization.

Employee Policies

Your employee will have a ton of questions about how things work at your company and what they should expect from you. These are all detailed in your employee policies. Things from vacation time, to employee evaluation, to communication practices, to dress code all need policies. A great third-party vendor for HR will have a good boilerplate employee policy handbook as a starter point. You need to take that foundation and infuse your culture into those policies to make them your own.

Compensation and Benefits

Compensation and benefits is an aspect of operations where the dependence on finance is pronounced. Operations is responsible for designing compensation packages for employees. Besides salary, packages include benefits like healthcare coverage, retirement investment accounts, and often also include stock grants. Your company does not exist in a vacuum. The competition is every other company in the world, including the one that your employee may want to start. Compensation and benefits is a huge part of HR and must be designed strategically, or it will be a constant distraction to the progress of your company.

Professional Development

One of the biggest aspects of HR that employees want but don't feel they get from the companies they work for is professional development. These days we expect an employee to stay at a company for only one to four years. It feels difficult as an employer to invest in an employee knowing that this investment will leave with that employee when they go. This differs from the work world fifty years ago when employees were expected to stay for decades. It was plausible that someone would start in the mailroom and through hard work and dedication, might one day rise to become the CEO of the company.

Times have changed. Today, any expectation that your employees will stay for a decade is laughable. Your employees' expectation of you, however, to provide professional development opportunities to them is very real and has become table stakes for talent acquisition. This is key to engagement, commitment to culture, and retention when there is always someone who can pay more salary than you.

Professional development is an opportunity for you to bring your culture to life and get more out of your employees. You can integrate it into the way you operate your company, so you never have to worry about how you are doing it. Here are some key opportunities to infuse professional development into the way your company operates:

- *Onboarding:* First impressions are huge. Onboarding is your opportunity to make an incredible first impression on your new employee. Through well-designed onboarding, you can make sure your new employee understands the culture of the organization, how things work, and how they will develop at the company while being successful at their job. How you do this is your creative opportunity, but understand that onboarding is where you set the tone for professional development.
- *Training and Certifications:* We live in an era where education is being disrupted. There are many inexpensive ways to use training and certifications that upgrade your employees for your company's benefits and develop them to become leaders in your company and more viable in the job market at the same time.
- *Management Interactions:* Design your regular one-on-one meetings and your employee assessment meetings around professional development. Corrective behavior should happen immediately, not once a week or once a year. Your scheduled touchpoints with your employees should generally be positive engagements they can

look forward to because you frame them around their success. Give your employees a solid assessment of where they are. Use these assessments to help them understand how they are progressing and how you will support them in their continued progression.

Conflict Resolution, Correcting Behavior, and Termination

I'll bucket the hard things together because most people don't like to address them, including me. But they have to be done. The better you are at communicating how your company operates regarding these tough issues, the easier it will be to deal with these situations as they arise. Conflict is inevitable. Not handling conflict can impact the health of your culture, the operations within your company, and can even get you in trouble with the law. Ever heard of wrongful termination?

Conflicts will happen at your company. It's a part of life, and when you are dealing with questions about how to deliver value for your customer, debates will arise. People are people and sometimes take things personally, act unprofessionally, and miscommunicate with or misunderstand their colleagues. The way to handle conflict both consistently and well is to have a clear, defined model that reflects your company's values for conflict resolution.

> Note: A fairly universal approach that works is addressing conflict with empathy, clarity, and without attacking a person's character or intent.

On correcting behavior and termination, talk to your attorney first. There will probably be documented steps that you have to follow according to the labor laws you are subject to that require some process to be followed. After that, apply your cultural values to your process and make it an authentic, caring experience. Everyone won't be successful at your company. Sometimes they won't have the ability to deliver. It's just as much your fault for hiring them as it is their fault for signing up for something they couldn't do.

> Note: One of the most important things to think about is how you communicate a termination to the rest of the company. People become fearful when being terminated, so be clear, honest, and open for feedback and questions when you have to remove someone from the organization.

Surprise and Delight

Believe it or not, your employees are your customers "in the building." You have to sell them on the idea that there is no place better in the world for them to be. The reason for this is selfish. Recruiting and hiring takes a lot of time and is expensive. It provides little value to the operations of your business. Yes, this is an investment. But every day you can keep an employee engaged and developing for your business is another day that you remove the risk of failure in the operation in your business. It's like maintenance for your car. Keep your employees tuned up and your business will run well.

Human Resources Is Huge

As soon as you bring in the first employee, you're on the hook for doing HR well. For most small businesses, an HR professional will not be your initial hire, so you will need to do it yourself. Your employees will evaluate your culture based on how you handle HR, not what you say during pep rally speeches. Hire a HR vendor and work with your attorney for compliance-oriented aspects of HR, but the things that make your culture unique are all on you.

Process, Technology, and Measurement

Once you've addressed the risks of compliance and employees, the final category of risk to address in operations is execution. When I say execution, I don't mean killing anything, I mean getting all the work done that needs to be done—meeting or exceeding the expectations of leadership.

In your budgets and projections, there are a lot of assumptions you made that need to come true in order for your business to meet or exceed projections. Failing to achieve those assumptions (e.g., items sold, cost of delivering service, renewals, etc.) puts your financial model at risk, and in case it's not clear, that's a bad thing.

You'll give yourself the best shot of making your financial model work by creating processes, leveraging technology, and measuring all the most important things that contribute to your assumptions for the business. As a general rule, keep things as simple as possible. Start by defining processes for all the key activities in your business.

Note: Be careful, this is an area where you have to be critical of yourself. It's easy to fall in love with process and avoid doing other critical aspects of the business. Shooting from the hip can mean that the business isn't repeatable and scalable. This requires judgment and constant evaluation by leadership to determine when something needs a process and when it should be implied.

Start by documenting each aspect of a job that an employee has to do. When you define the processes that an employee needs to follow to get their job done, you create clarity, alignment of expectations, and the ability to delegate work. You can also assess an employee's work. Either they adhered to the process or not. Simple.

We can implement most processes with technology these days. Technology provides additional structure to a process, and can create audit trails for the activity of employees and vendors against the prescribed processes for the business. An example of this is sales and a customer relationship management (CRM) system like Salesforce, HubSpot, or Pipedrive.

In high-touch, high-dollar sales, it's critical to have a process for qualifying a potential customer. You want to deploy the right level of engagement to the potential customer (often called a prospect in sales terms) at the right time. CRMs have formalized this process with a tool called a pipeline. A pipeline captures sales activity in a reporting structure that enables salespeople to place prospects in the right categories of qualification, so management can see how their team is doing in terms of activity, adhering to the process and results.

One of the greatest venture capitalists of all time, John Doerr, wrote a great book about measurement called *Measure What Matters*. In it, he introduces the concept of OKRs, which stands for Objectives and Key Results. While OKRs are not the only model for defining what we should measure in a business, it's been adopted by some of the most successful companies in the world. I recommend reading it for insight on how to define what the objectives and key results are within your business, and how you should measure them.

The combination of process, leveraging technology to

strengthen the process, and measuring key aspects of the process is critical to addressing execution risk. You can see how it impacts everything downstream of operations. Internal communications, customer support, marketing, etc. all need processes, technology to support those processes, and clear models of measurement to determine if execution is on target or suboptimal.

That wraps up my overview on Operations. You can see how much Operations will influence the areas of Growth, Product, Service, Sales, and Marketing in your business. All of those aspects will have contracts that govern how they engage with all stakeholders. If you are successful enough to grow, there will be employees for each of these aspects of the business, and HR will be critical to how those employees are engaged. All aspects of your business need process, technology, and measurement to ensure that the assumptions of how your business operates are realized.

Again, aligning all operations around the vision and values of the company, and ensuring this through great management is the trick of making a company operate well. Operations, like all other parts of a business, is an exercise in leadership.

GROWTH

Operating a business forces you to accept reality. One reality of business is that you always have competition. That competition could be another company offering a similar product or service. It could also be *status quo*. Sometimes the customer doesn't know that what you are offering has value or they have a different way of getting the value that you are trying to deliver. When an entrepreneur says they have no competition, they fail to acknowledge the reality of business and are setting themselves up for failure.

One of the most important realities to accept about business is that change is always happening, and it will impact every part of your business. Every part. You don't have to design your business to grow. However it's much easier to address change if you design for growth, because *choosing to grow means you choose to drive change as opposed to being subject to it*. Trying to maintain your business as-is means you will always be on the receiving end of change. That will negatively impact the health of the business.

Growth is the **optimization of your business.** Growth does not require you to add more employees. In fact, growth can often be about doing more with less. Growth does mean constantly seeking to improve. *Growth is about understanding that change is always happening. You can and should drive and leverage change to realize the vision and live out the values of the company.*

The tech titans—Amazon, Facebook, Google, and Apple—

have done an incredible job of driving growth to achieve their vision and live out their values. The hallmarks of smart growth are *reinvestment, anticipation, and innovation.*

REINVESTMENT

A critical mistake (that I've made over and over) in preparing for growth, is failing to commit to reinvestment. Rather than pulling out as much profit as possible in the business, plan on reinvesting a significant amount of the profit in the business to grow the business. Reinvestment has many incredible benefits and can be done in different ways, but the key is to commit to a significant reinvestment strategy.

What can you do with a reinvestment strategy?

- Build a war chest for acquiring other companies.
- Increase your compensation standards, which would help you attract better talent and keep your top talent.
- Increase your marketing budget to grow demand for your business.
- Make significant investments in technology and operations that will allow you to control more of your operations and lower the cost of operations.

These moves will better position your company to control its future in a market where change is an ever-present variable. Growing your market share, improving and getting more out of your workforce, and creating new product lines are ways to offset negative change elements that could be in store for your business. Reinvestment is the principle that allows you to do that and grow.

ANTICIPATION

Look at the market and have a vision about where the market will be in the future. Your growth strategy can't be taking your existing financial model and increasing it every year. You must anticipate that some change, probably driven by innovation, will change the way business will be done in your industry. You have to run through various scenarios of change and ask yourself, "How will my business operate when the fundamentals of doing business as I know them change?"

If you do that, you can put growth strategies in place to leverage your strengths and evolve where needed to continue to grow in the face of the change.

INNOVATION

The boldest, bravest way to lean into growth and to drive change is by embracing innovation. It's also proving to be the smartest way to do it.

In 2005, the largest companies in the world were energy

and finance conglomerates like Exxon Mobil, General Electric, BP, Citigroup, and Bank of America. Today, they are still conglomerates, but they are all technology companies whose most defensible asset is their ability to innovate. Apple, Alphabet (Google), Amazon, Facebook, and Microsoft are now the biggest, most valuable companies in the world. The reason? They are driving change through innovation.

It's incredible that twentieth century incumbent companies can watch iconic peers like GE, Sears, Toys"R"Us, the entire newspaper industry and more, lose to innovative new entrants and still ignore the direct connection between innovation and growth. It's willful ignorance, but you don't have to follow their lead. Whether you are leading a large incumbent or you are starting your first business, know that innovation is now a constant reality of our world. Make it a core competency of your business if you want to optimize your ability to achieve your company's vision.

GROWTH IS ABOUT ACCEPTING CHANGE AND DRIVING IT

There is no middle ground here. You are either growing or you are shrinking. You may be slowly shrinking, but the economy does not allow businesses to hold where they are without ambition. Small businesses aren't safe from the tech titans, and most employees aren't loyal anymore.

Customers expect that the market will fight for their business, that they deserve the best for their money, and that the bar on what "the best" looks like will be raised every year. Growth is a mentality that optimization is the only way to stay in business, and it's a never-ending process. You can grow forever, just ask Amazon.

A SOLID FOUNDATION

That covers the four internal core concepts and gives you a sense of how much work has to go into leadership inside the building. Entrepreneurs, especially early in their careers, are eager and impatient. But as with all things, a business cannot be built on a shoddy foundation. Become a lifelong student of leadership, finance, operations, and growth, and you will only become a more potent entrepreneur as you progress in your journey.

CHAPTER SIX

* * *

THE EIGHT CORE CONCEPTS PART II: OUTSIDE THE BUILDING

A CHAPTER ABOUT BUSINESS IN ACTION

If your house is in order, you can compete in the market with confidence. The concepts outside the building are simple compared to the concepts inside the building, because they leverage them. There is also so much variation in implementation of the outside concepts that I'll only cover their most universal aspects. From here on, everything gets customer-centric.

PRODUCT

Silicon Valley has taken the term *product* and created a

new paradigm out of it. I've been in the technology space for most of my career and I continue to find the Valley's definition of *product* confusing and hard to communicate. Depending on who you listen to in the market, *product* should cover a deep understanding of the customer, pricing, packaging, delivery, support, and on and on and on.

I've found that the easiest way for me to understand product is to get back to its original meaning. A product is **a predictable unit of value.** There is a lot to unpack in the term "predictable unit of value." Let's start there and see if we can try to make sense of the evolving definition of product that Silicon Valley is driving.

PREDICTABLE

According to Merriam-Webster, predictable means: "as one would expect."

A customer has an expectation of what they will receive from you. Remember, they have a job to do. They are choosing to work with you to help them get their job done. And they have expectations about how you will help them get their job done. Your job is to meet (or exceed) their expectations, period. If you are predictable, you will succeed. If not, then you will fail. This is binary. Predictability is a key hallmark of product, and the buck stops here on ensuring that the experience of the customer is predictably awesome.

UNIT

Unit is key to product because it puts boundaries around the expectations that the customer has of the company helping them to get their job done. According to Merriam-Webster, unit means: "a single quantity regarded as a whole in calculation."

A unit is the *whole amount* of what the customer expects you to do to help them get their job done that can enable a transaction. One tire, one hot dog, one shirt, one software license, one song, one logo, one hour of cleaning. Whatever can make up a single quantity that can be seen as complete and fit for transaction, is a unit.

Units are what your customer expects to get from you, and units are core to your financial model as they are the object that you base costs and pricing against. Units are what the customer will give you money for, and you must be able to deliver that unit to the customer at a profit, predictably. Units give us a basis upon which to determine value.

VALUE

Value is the final part of the product definition. According to Merriam-Webster, value means: "the monetary worth of something."

Value is a term from economics and is driven by supply and

demand. If supply is high and demand doesn't outpace supply, then the value of the unit will be low, because there is excess supply around. If the demand outpaces the supply, then the value can go up. The former scenario means that the profit margins will be low on the product, whereas the latter scenario results in higher margin products.

What's interesting (and not obvious) in this analysis of value, is that demand isn't linear for all products in a category. A clear example of this is Apple's iPhone. There are hundreds of cell phone models on the market today, and they all enable a person to make calls to other phones. But the iPhone is something more than just a cell phone.

The expectations that customers have of iPhones are higher than the expectations customers have of any other phone. That's because iPhones are a particular kind of cell phone, with an enhanced value proposition that puts them in a class by themselves. Since Apple is the only source of supply of iPhones in the market, Apple can charge more for them than other cell phone makers can charge for their cell phones.

Now that we've covered what a product is, I'd like to offer a bit of commentary.

The Silicon Valley definition of product leaves many entrepreneurs out of the conversation, and that's bullshit.

Whether you base your business on the internet or fashion or hospitality or farming, you can always distill your product down to a predictable unit of value, and that should remain the universal definition of product.

I'm about to get into the concept of service. Some people separate product-based businesses from service-based businesses, and I think this is misguided. Service-based businesses are the same as product-based businesses in that the customer expects a unit of value that they will get for their money. This idea that service-based businesses don't play by the same rules as product-based businesses needs to be debunked.

Let's look at graphic design for example. For a long time, graphic designers charged their clients an hourly rate to deliver a result, and customers dealt with that because they had little to no alternatives. Then a company called 99 Designs emerged and created predictable units of value, like logo designs for $199. Using a global workforce of designers who agreed to these terms, 99 Designs took a lot of market share away from graphic designers who charged an hourly fee.

The market doesn't lie. Customers always want a predictable unit of value in exchange for their money. Attorneys, accountants, mechanics, and other service-based businesses are on the brink of disruption because they see themselves as different from product-based businesses even though their customers don't. Customers don't have a product-based bank account and a service-based bank account. To customers, money is money, and they hate surprises that make them feel they can't know for sure what they are getting for their money.

Every company needs to think like a product-based company to have a healthy relationship with their customers.

SERVICE

Service humanizes relationships between the customer and the company. The customer buys a product to receive value, but they want to be treated as valuable by the company. As an entrepreneur, your goal is to create a happy customer. Much of this responsibility lies in your product's quality and efficacy. But a further expectation is that you will show your appreciation for your customer's business and help them when unexpected problems arise. Service is how you do that. Service is your company's ability to **maximize customer satisfaction.**

WHAT COULD GO WRONG?

Products will be defective from time to time. Deliveries will fail to arrive as expected. Occasionally your product will suddenly stop performing as you promised it would. You can count on your customer misunderstanding the features of what they bought from you. Sometimes you didn't do anything wrong but your customer is just having a bad day. Believe it or not, your customer might make a mistake in their use of your product and blame you for it.

How does your business respond to this and the million other scenarios that could impact the satisfaction of your customer? Service.

You should build the cost of good service into the price of your product, but make no mistake, it's not the same as your product. Service is something you do on top of delivering the product. Your product should do the job of delivering the predictable unit of value to the customer on its own. Service should make a satisfied customer a raving fan, and bring a dissatisfied customer back to being satisfied.

GUARANTEE

There is one word that you can use to give your business an advantage over your competitors: guarantee. The thing about a guarantee is it can't be an afterthought. You have to build a guarantee into your business model, your financial model, and probably in some way in your vision and values. If you do, you set a standard for the level of service you will deliver to your customer that your entire organization is committed to and can support viably.

Always try to offer some kind of guarantee if it is reasonable for your business. It makes your commitment valuable to your customer and empowers your service organization. That's the entire purpose of service. It's simple: take care of your customer.

SALES

Sales is what your company does to make a person give you money for a product they want. For an online retailer, this looks like an e-commerce site. For a car company, this looks like a salesperson on the lot who spends time with the customer, takes them on a test drive, and helps them with all the paperwork that has to be completed. In a consulting business, this looks like creating a proposal, negotiating with the customer over the details of a proposal, and getting them to sign a contract. At a grocery store, this is having all the products the customer wants on the shelves, and enabling them to check out and pay for everything they want before they leave.

Sales is about **generating revenue** by assisting and enabling the transaction between a customer and your business to happen.

The sales process requires a complete knowledge of the product that the company is offering, and needs to be defined by the service standards and criteria that the company has set. Sales is a revenue-focused activity, period. Sales drives revenue for the business in a way that is consistent with the vision and values of the company. Sales has to hit the financial goals that the company has set.

Sales has to follow processes and be measurable. Sales is almost always the place where growth ambitions are most pronounced, because it takes revenue to grow a business. These days sales doesn't necessarily require salespeople. Plenty of online businesses generate significant revenue without a single salesperson. But sales require that your business communicates the price of the product and the terms of service to your customer, and then takes their money and delivers the product they purchased.

Sales can be as complicated or simple as the product you sell and the service you offer. If you are selling a complex product that costs a lot of money, the sales process will be intensive and cost a lot of money. If the product is simple, like a book, then your sales process can be simple and inexpensive to execute. Sales packages your product and service and generates revenue for your company by completing the transaction with the customer.

MARKETING

Marketing is my favorite concept, even though it is the last of the eight, because it is the most comprehensive. It takes all the previous concepts, and engages every single day with the market at large to validate all the assumptions the company has made. Marketing can't fix a broken financial model or dysfunctional operations. Marketing can't help a company with an unclear vision or that doesn't live up to its values. Marketing can't overcome a product that does not deliver value or a terrible standard of service or a poor sales process. Marketing is a mirror of the truth for the business. It **identifies, understands, and (*if possible*) generates demand**.

BRAND

Marketing has the distinct honor of being the keeper of a company's brand. A company's brand is what a customer thinks of when they think of your company. Marketers package the company's vision, values, product, and service into visual and audible messages that communicate across any medium to help the customer identify the company.

Brand is powerful. If it is packaged well and communicated well, it can ignite the most effective and oldest form of marketing in the world—word of mouth. People trust other people who have the same job to do as them, to recommend a company to help them get that job done.

By leveraging brand, marketing can do what none of the other concepts can. Marketing creates awareness to potential customers who don't yet know about your company. There are so many tactics with which to do that—pre-internet tactics like word of mouth, radio, newspaper, magazines, billboards, television, and more. These tactics all work to create awareness but are difficult to track just how effective they are. The internet revolutionized marketing by making just about every aspect of the marketing process trackable. This has changed the entire business landscape for two reasons:

1. Customer attention has shifted from non-digital mediums to digital mediums because of the internet and specifically, social networks. This means that businesses now have to engage with customers on these platforms, which is powerful, but also much more complex because the communication is two-way.
2. The ever-changing marketing landscape means that marketing requires a bigger investment than it ever has before. Not just an investment in money, but time to constantly learn and master it.

The upside of this shift to digital is that marketing has become a much more intelligent discipline. Marketing is now the trusted voice of the customer for many companies. In order for this to permeate throughout your organization, marketing has to have integration points and feedback loops throughout. Marketing needs to work hand in hand with sales, service, and product teams. It also needs to have a direct channel to leadership, so leaders can understand how the customer is interpreting and responding to the vision that the company espouses.

Social networks have given customers a platform to broadcast their opinions of companies in a way they never had before. This is a game changer. Marketers can use this to better listen to the market. What are customers saying about their company, about their company's competitors, and about the job they need to get done? Marketers have so much power at their disposal because of the internet, but they also have so much more responsibility now.

Marketing has to be experimental by testing copy, imagery, targeting, and channel combinations for desktops, laptops, tablets, and phones. It's a brave new world. Marketing, in the age of internet, is both a driver of demand and a validator of value that helps companies correct issues faster than ever before. Marketing is not magic; it can't overcome failures upstream in the business. But it can identify those failures faster than ever before, and can help deliver service to resolve those failures.

Marketing depends on all other concepts, but it is the most comprehensive and customer-facing of them.

USING THE FRAMEWORK

If you are anything like me, being an entrepreneur is fun because at least one of these core concepts is fun for you. I liked parts of operations because I liked technology, and I really enjoyed marketing because it was constantly changing. I learned through face-plant after face-plant that the other concepts were not only critical, but were often more critical than the ones I loved.

To get the most out of this framework, you need the discipline to work comprehensively. The framework of the Eight Core Concepts is simple and complete and will give you the ability to reverse engineer any existing business to build a blueprint of your own. I hope you find it useful.

CHAPTER SEVEN

* * *

WHAT GOOD LEADERS DO

A CHAPTER ABOUT CREATING CULTURE

Peter Drucker famously said, "Culture eats strategy for breakfast." His point was that no matter how smart you are, your company's culture sets the limits of what's possible, not the quality of your ideas. That's why it's worth dedicating an entire chapter to the importance of culture, and how hard it can be to get it right.

I CAN TELL YOU A LOT ABOUT HOW NOT TO BUILD COMPANY CULTURE

In 2008, I was building out Remarkable Wit (RW) and as I've already shared in chapter 4, my wife and I were going through a divorce. When I started RW, my goal was to bring what Emma did so well into my new venture—culture. As

I started to hire people, I found that the things I thought made up a company's culture were only surface-level accessories. I may have experienced the Emma culture, but I never took the time to ask Clint and Will how they actually created it. Happy hours, impromptu breaks in the middle of the workday, and creative side projects were the tools I had in my toolbox to build a "cool" culture.

These were tactics, they weren't the culture itself. The tactics were fun but did little to address the challenges that RW would encounter, and that's what you need a strong culture for. What's crazy is, I thought the tactics were special, and got upset at the employees for not being grateful for the "culture" we had. My failure to craft a vision and a set of values and reinforce them every day would make every significant challenge we faced as a team almost impossible to overcome.

Establishing and consistently communicating a vision and values with your team gives them a framework for how to work with and support each other when you aren't around. When vision and values aren't there, it leaves your team to their individual skills and habits to address the inevitable conflicts that arise. That can cause serious fractures in your company.

As our workload increased, managing multiple projects at the same time, it put stress on our team to deliver. If I knew what I was doing, I would have recognized that the growth we were experiencing required a rethinking of the business and financial model. But that wasn't the case. I didn't understand enough about finance and operations to ensure that I didn't overwork my team, so of course, I overworked them. An overworked team is a stressed out and unhappy team. Stress and unhappiness breed conflict and test any organization.

To address the growth pains we were experiencing, I put one of the team members in an internal leadership position so I could focus on the customers. Because I didn't establish vision and values, I put this person in an almost impossible situation for success. Once I took the time to watch what was happening inside the building, the entire team was at odds with the guy I put in leadership. He predictably failed at getting them through stressful periods, and to keep the team intact, I had to terminate him. This was devastating for me and was a sign of more bad things to come.

The client project that was creating the most stress for us was an online marketplace for knowledge called Moontoast. We were building Moontoast for its co-founders for cash and some equity. It was an ambitious project, pushing the boundaries of what technology was available at the time for internet applications. What started as a great showcase deal for RW in revenue and equity ended up being the deal that killed RW. Another failure of leadership, stemming from my inexperience, was not knowing how much leverage I gave them as a customer, because they grew to become 70 percent of our revenue. Seems obvious, but I didn't do enough to produce new client revenue to decrease their leverage over us.

After almost a year of working on Moontoast, the co-founders needed more funding to get the project launched. They ran out of friends and family to raise money from, and it was time to find a real venture capitalist to fund the company. I had no experience with venture capital at that point as Emma's founders only relied on a bank loan to get the company off the ground. I was about to get schooled on how bad things can get when you don't have leverage in a venture capital transaction. The co-founders and I went to Charlie Martin, a very successful healthcare entrepreneur who was starting his own venture fund, and was interested in the vision of Moontoast.

The negotiations started out well. But as Charlie learned more about the state of the company and the nature of the relationship between Moontoast and Remarkable Wit, he built some aggressive terms into the deal. First, his investment would give his firm a controlling stake in the company. Second, I would have to join the company full time as chief technology officer. Third, I had to move my development team from Remarkable Wit to Moontoast, and fire all the other Remarkable Wit employees. I had no choice but to comply; I had no walkaway leverage.

In case you didn't get it by now, what I did was not what good leaders do.

I spent four years in a variety of C-level roles at Moontoast as an employee with a single digit equity stake. By the end of those four years, none of the original Remarkable Wit team that came with me was still at Moontoast. Our software platform pivoted from an eBay-like marketplace for knowledge to a Facebook interactive ad software as a service platform serving the music, auto, and CPG industries.

We had great wins with some of the biggest consumer companies in the world like Universal Music Group, P&G, and Toyota, and made some significant, patented innovations at Moontoast. However some of our strategic decisions proved terrible and doomed the company. The biggest one was that our business was dependent on Facebook, and one day, Facebook changed their strategy and it killed our business. Millions of dollars in revenue went away as Facebook no longer supported our product. We were done.

We weren't alone. Moontoast was one of a hundred companies called Facebook Preferred Marketing Developers that were inventing solutions on top of Facebook. A ton of venture capital had gone into these companies, and a bunch of smart people poured themselves into what they thought would be an ecosystem of value. What we all learned was that Facebook didn't exist to create value for us. It existed to create value for its shareholders. They took back all the business they were sending to us, and almost all those Facebook Preferred Marketing Developers are now out of business. The lesson? The same as my 70 percent revenue lesson with RW and Moontoast. Never give up too much leverage.

I could write an entire chapter about the leadership challenges we had at Moontoast. But the easiest way to summarize it is that our leadership team never could establish a unified vision and values and model them. Even though we were well funded and had assembled a team of talented people, our ability to align our team and get them to support each other was not there. If the Remarkable Wit experience gave me a glimpse into the importance of good leadership, the Moontoast experience hammered the point home and changed me forever. After Moontoast, I became critical of myself as a leader and a student of leadership development.

WHAT SHOULD WE SAY OF WHAT GOOD LEADERS DO?

It's no small task to determine what good leadership looks like. The topic of leadership is as old as philosophy and religion itself, and we can find commentary on it in the most revered cultural texts in the world. This book contains my thoughts on the fundamentals of entrepreneurship, but there may be none more important than those on leadership. I have strong opinions on what good leadership looks like.

In chapter 5, I distilled the entire purpose of leadership down to the creation and reinforcement of culture. Culture is a complex word. In the context of a business, think of culture as the prescribed practices of communication, collaboration, working style, and philosophy on competition of the organization. A good leader takes time to think through what their organization's culture is and what it is not, and memorializes it with affirmations and narrative. A good leader models the actions that reflect the culture as they have defined it. When culture is intentionally designed and reinforced, the organization feels aligned and like it's destined to perform.

Good leaders inspire, mentor, and cultivate other good leaders. As I've come in contact with leaders of organizations, it has shocked me how often mentoring and succession planning is not part of the organization's focus. Perhaps it stems from some growing sense of mortality, but I am always thinking about how my organizations will go on without me.

The succession and mentoring path does not come organically. It is something that requires focus and intention. Intentionally working towards a day when you are no longer the most critical person on your team is what good leaders do. And this is hard work. Inspiring, mentoring, and cultivating others taps into the heart of what it means to be human. This is not simply about managing people. Developing leaders is a much more primal, essential act.

Good leaders touch people, they change people, they remember that they are dealing with people, and that emotion is always at play. Good leaders remain aware of the impact they have on people and understand they have a responsibility to those they lead.

In small organizations, the relationship between a leader and those they lead can be as intense as a close friendship. Some organizations are so large that they base the relationship on the images and words the leader projects because the leader can't touch all they lead. In either case, what the leader does impacts and influences those who they lead, and the good leader understands this.

Mentorship takes time but has a multiplying effect on the strength of the organization, and so it's one of the most important things a good leader can do. Each person mentored by a good leader has a much better chance of becoming a leader and doing the same for another person in the organization. The leader multiplies the essential aspects of themselves when they mentor. It's not a carbon copy, it's better than that. It's a manifestation of the principles of the organization imprinted on someone besides yourself with their own unique skills and talents.

Good leaders work hard at being good leaders and that work never stops. They study leadership. They understand that leadership is a discipline. You can't lead others if you can't lead yourself. That means guiding yourself to make the best decisions you can and treating yourself accordingly when you fall short.

When falling short, which we will, we must be careful not to berate ourselves to the point of sustained negative energy. We need to learn from the mistakes we make, but we need to keep them in perspective.

There are mistakes and there are showstoppers. Showstoppers are terrible decisions that irrevocably change things for the worse. Showstoppers deserve serious warning. Everything else deserves guidance but not too much warning. If we don't reserve serious responses for the dangerous situations, how will we know to take the warnings for showstoppers seriously?

Good leaders are honest with themselves. Authenticity is something people can feel, and good leaders are authentic. With authenticity comes trust, and good leaders are effective because they build trust with people, which quickens the pace of their impact in the organization.

If we are honest with ourselves, we must admit that we are not always right. Good leaders know that and accept that those they lead know that. Therefore, good leaders are not beyond reproach. Good leaders welcome questions about their direction, and have answers based in reason, principle, ethics, logic, and strategy. Good leaders admit when they are wrong and apologize when they make mistakes that impact their people.

HOW TO LEAD WHEN YOU DON'T HAVE EXPERIENCE AS A LEADER

Part of why leadership is associated with experience is that it's difficult to lead through things you've never encountered. It's not impossible, but it's difficult. For example, the first time I had to fire someone was a gut-wrenching experience. Since that day, I've been more thoughtful about who I hire and how.

Experience, however, cannot be the key ingredient of leadership for several important reasons. First, leaders chart new territory and explore possibilities that have not yet been documented. How then do you lead people into and through the unknown? In my experience, the key is to combine care for those you lead and adherence to a set of principles that give you direction and steadfastness.

Another problem with overvaluing experience for leaders

is that it reflects one of the key challenges of any organization: bias. Experience shapes perspective in ways that are both good and bad. It's important to always accept new perspectives as a leader. Experience is helpful when it exposes patterns of cause and effect that less experienced members of your team miss. It is less helpful when it closes you off to ideas foreign to you. Too often we value that which we know over that which we don't understand.

Therefore, experience is valuable but not required for leadership. I say this to liberate you. If you don't have experience in leadership yet, that does not mean you cannot become a leader. Experience as a leader will not make you immune from mistakes, so you are better off getting started and making them now.

COMMUNICATION IS THE JOB

Is there any action more core to leadership than communication? Good leaders connect their people to "the big picture." When a good leader communicates, their people can relay the message to others with minimal alterations, so that message can spread. Communication happens via many mediums—one-on-one, in a group meeting, as a speaker at an event, digitally, etc. A good leader thinks about how to communicate across all mediums.

When new CEOs complain about challenges they face in

their organization, I say to them, "You are the chief communication officer first, then the chief executive officer." In the twenty-first century, social media has ensured that no person and no leader is beyond reproach. The mindset that lingers from past centuries implies that a leader can simply direct from a position of command versus inspire from a position of influence, but that mindset no longer exists. Today, to be an effective leader, you must work diligently to inspire and engender trust when you communicate. This will enable you to use commands when necessary and have your words carry weight.

Any leader can learn to improve their communication skills if they work at it. It is a well-studied discipline with incredible scientific research poured into it. There are whole advanced degrees dedicated to the topic. You can never stop improving how well you communicate. It's your number one tool for leveling up your ability as a leader.

Here are seven keys to leadership communication that you can begin working on to improve your communication skills today.

ATTENTION

Everyone values when people pay attention to them. It's a fundamental desire that humans have. As a leader, you can communicate more effectively with your team by showing them they are worthy of your attention. A practical way to do this is to schedule one-on-one time with those who most need your input and your ear. The committed amount of time and frequency is always relative to how much you need to invest in the person. Scheduling time with someone gives them a sense that communicating with them is a priority.

LISTENING

The best leaders ask thoughtful questions and listen. You learn more that way and listening conveys to your team that gathering insight is important to you. All the people in your organization will both respect you more and be more honest with you if they know you for your ability to listen. You will learn so much about your organization by being a good, attentive listener.

REPETITION

As a young leader, I was often upset with my team over how many times I needed to say something in order for it to "sink in." Over time, I became more attuned to my role as a communicator and I realized if someone didn't get what I was saying, that was my fault. Remember, the leader has to be accountable for the outcome, always. Good leaders understand the need to say the same thing, many times to the same group of people, making sure everyone understands what they are communicating. As a general rule, one time is never enough.

EMPATHY

In the twenty-first century, leaders are required to communicate across three generations: baby boomers, Generation X, and millennials. The ability to communicate with this multigenerational audience effectively is challenging. What motivates these different generations can often be very different. I don't enjoy generalizing what motivates generations, but it's true that they grew up in different times with different values. You must accept that one message won't touch all people because of these differences.

Empathy is the state of understanding and sharing another person's experiences and emotions. Using empathy can help you understand your audience and be more effective as a communicator. The better in tune you are with your team's feelings, the more you will interpret their nonverbal communication. Things like body language, digital communication, and patterns in performance are all much easier to decipher if you have developed empathy for your people.

Emotions play a powerful role in one's performance. I question any leader who doesn't believe tapping into and understanding the emotions of their team is a critical part of their ability to communicate with them.

STICK WITH VISION

It is the leader's job to look out over the horizon and see what is coming and guide their organization into the future. This is a critical job for the leader, anchoring to the vision and using it to guide people through change. If a leader doesn't continue to work at this strategic level, it will limit the level of leadership they can achieve.

MAKING DECISIONS

Leaders face choices every day. Decision-making is a hallmark of leadership. Indecisiveness communicates insecurity about your ability to lead. People expect leaders to make decisions, and if fear of making the wrong decision paralyzes you, you will lose the confidence of those you lead. Here are three keys to the skill of making decisions that every leader must develop so you can make decisions and convey them confidently:

1. Understanding deadlines. It's important to have clarity around how long one can take before deciding. Leaders must know when to act swiftly versus when they can be patient and communicate those deadlines so everyone else understands when to expect a decision.
2. Gathering background. You'll want to know how much information you need before you can make a solid decision. Significant decisions such as budget allocation,

bringing on a new hire, or committing to a long-term strategy require a lot of information.

3. Developing a framework. Sometimes there are decisions laid before us that we can't process and have to make from the gut. Most of the time, decisions can be made using a framework of qualifying questions around benefit and risk. Good leaders understand the benefit of a framework, so they save their gut for only the most challenging decisions. Having a framework allows you to communicate how you make decisions, which gives people clarity and empowers them to make decisions in the same way you would.

MANAGE EMOTIONS

As a leader with the primary job of communicating effectively to your team, you must manage your emotions. This means you shouldn't overreact to others' emotions. You cannot allow your own emotions to get out of control. You must manage your own emotions in public. The hard work of being a leader is absorbing others' emotional reactions, while maintaining an example of what leadership looks like in your response.

Everyone needs a space where they can be vulnerable, honest, and emotional, including leaders. But in front of those you lead is almost never that place. Sometimes it's appropriate to remind people you are human and show them how you feel to create a deeper connection with you. But these situations lose their impact if they happen too often. Be thoughtful about when you show your emotions with your team.

Good leaders know their people are always watching them, looking for cues on how the organization is doing through verbal and nonverbal communication. Therefore, all emotions that the leader expresses must be managed to respect that fact and keep the organization stable and moving forward through positive communications.

Attention, Listening, Repetition, Empathy, Vision, Making Decisions and Managing Emotions. The seven keys to leadership communication that I see good leaders excel in.

CREATING, COMMUNICATING AND CULTIVATING THE CULTURE

The beauty of leadership is that while it isn't easy (in fact it's very hard), it is simple. Vision and values establish the framework for your culture. If you miss this, you miss everything. Once these are created, you must communicate and cultivate this culture every day. You must work on yourself, always becoming a better version of yourself, orchestrating across the Eight Core Concepts in your enterprise. Do that to the best of your ability, and you will never fail, you will only win or learn.

CHAPTER EIGHT

* * *

DON'T BELIEVE YOUR OWN PRESS

A CHAPTER ABOUT FOCUSING ON WHAT MATTERS

Seeing your name in lights can be blinding. As the leader of your company, you have to stay grounded and remember that customers keep the lights on, not headlines.

AND THE WINNER IS...

In 2009, the Nashville Technology Council (NTC) nominated Moontoast for "Startup Company of the Year." It was a major boost to my confidence after a year of turmoil and the significant struggle to fold Remarkable Wit into Moontoast. We accumulated some clients, built a technology platform, and we were doing good work. It was something to be proud of.

However, I got obsessed with the nomination. I developed strong feelings of entitlement about the years I spent contributing to Nashville's technology community and that this nomination was my deserved recognition for that. But not just the recognition, the award itself. I became obsessed with the award.

Our company was up against just one other company in the category, CredenceHealth, a company that worked with healthcare providers to lower costs and improve clinical outcomes. I undervalued the importance of the healthcare sector in Nashville, which was a sign of my immaturity. Since I had heard little of this company, I went in thinking we had this award in the bag.

Note: By now, you should be cringing at the self-absorbed nature of this story and my part in it. I'm not proud of it, but it happened, and I think most of us can fall susceptible to it. That's why I'm sharing it.

The NTC awards arrived and after five categories of awards were announced, it was time to find out who the Startup of the Year would be. Justin Lanning, CredenceHealth's CEO, and I both walked on stage for the reveal of the award winner. "And the winner is...CredenceHealth!"

I took a large gulp, turned to Justin to shake his hand and congratulate him, and walked off stage right. I bit my lip for the rest of the night.

The event ended and everyone headed out for drinks.

After two cocktails, I went off. In particular, I went off on Tod Fetherling, the CEO of the Nashville Technology Council. He was my first client at Remarkable Wit and a good friend, so he let me vent, called me a cab, and put me in it. My girlfriend of less than a year, Rachel, was with me for the whole night and had to endure the embarrassing spectacle.

For the following years, I allowed this loss to put me into a fever for recognition. Capturing attention from the press and garnering awards became a goal for me. At Moontoast, this dysfunctional behavior continued. Moontoast was regularly featured in Nashville's local publications, *The Tennessean* and the *Nashville Business Journal*, and also covered by national publications like *Adweek* and *Billboard*. We were one of *Billboard's* top ten music startups in 2011. I've still got that magazine cover hanging up in my office.

We won many Facebook innovation awards over the years, and these were in fact helpful for brand recognition in the market. However, the problem was that I spent too much energy on recognition and not enough on execution. This is a confession I've never made before, but it is one of my greatest contributions to the shortcomings of Moontoast as a company. I cared too much about recognition. I cared too much about what other people thought about me.

CredenceHealth, the company that beat Moontoast for Startup Company of the Year in 2009, was acquired by Xerox in 2011. They deserved the honor. Moontoast did not achieve the acquisition that we sought after. I can't say that it was only because we were too focused on our press, but it's impossible to ignore how much energy we wasted focusing on it.

What's the point of this story? It's bigger than just placing too much emphasis on the press. It's about focusing on what others say about you, period. Recognition is a false indicator. Press and awards are tools to be leveraged, not measuring sticks for your accomplishments. But they are very seductive for entrepreneurs, and when an entrepreneur overvalues them, it means that underneath it all, they are insecure. I was. I was trying to compensate for the failure that RW was, and that I hadn't forgiven myself for it.

LET'S GET REAL ABOUT PRESS AND AWARDS

So here's the deal with press coverage and awards. I won't say they mean nothing, but they are 100 percent secondary to the actual health of your business.

For example, let's say Moontoast had won Startup of the

Year from the NTC in 2009. Seriously, what the hell does that even mean? Are we *actually* the best startup in Nashville? And, if so, is that why we created the company? Was it our vision to be the best startup in Nashville? Is that why everyone was working their asses off? Of course not. Who starts a company with the primary vision of winning an award or being on a list in some publication? No one.

What matters is whether or not your company is hitting its goals for the quarter. How much attention and energy are you putting into that? If you are focusing on what other people are saying about you, the answer is not enough.

Until this point in the book, I've shared my shortcomings. Don't worry, I'm about to shift into some wins. I'm sharing these losses because I learned so much from them that made me who I am today. I'm OK with you knowing that I failed, for years, on the path to experiencing success as an entrepreneur. And I know that I'm not done with the losses either. Win or learn.

SOCIAL MEDIA UPS THE ANTE

In 2009, my obsession was limited to awards and press recognition, because social media was just starting to take off. Today, social media fosters the debilitating habit of overvaluing others' opinions instead of measuring what matters. Everyone has an opinion, and with social media, everyone has a platform to broadcast that opinion. So focusing on what actually matters, matters now more than ever.

To communicate our value to the market, we will likely need to be engaged on social media. This will expose us to feedback of others, 24/7/365. Knowing this, being mentally strong will now be even more important to stay focused on what matters. Whether it's press, awards, or @heather82 on Twitter, filter what others say about you to help you better achieve your goals.

Establish a system so that when you have an emotional response to market feedback or press coverage, you can process it in a way that is productive and additive to your purpose. What does this mean, practically?

Let's say someone is saying something positive about you. This could be an award nomination or win, showing up on a prestigious list, or getting positive feedback from a customer. You might create a system on how you leverage that positive feedback for your strategic purposes:

- Have a way to take that praise and use it in marketing campaigns
- Communicate it to your team and use it to reinforce the good work they are doing
- Share the success with existing customers, thanking them for their support and the opportunity to do good work

Now let's look at the opposite scenario where the publicity or feedback about you is bad. This could be an article that is critical of the company, showing up on a not so desirable list (those exist too) or getting negative feedback from a customer. Once you assess the feedback, if you determine the feedback is justified, you could respond humbly, showing your values and commitment to learning from mistakes and always getting better:

- Have a communications policy where you, as the leader, respond within a certain amount of time and accept the failure and commit to improve
- Communicate it to your team and use it as an opportunity to model how to handle negative feedback and use it as motivation to improve
- Communicate to existing customers honestly and commit to always improve and acknowledge where you have fallen short
- Determine with the key people on your team what failure of execution created the situation and come up with a plan to ensure that it doesn't happen again

The specifics of the plan aren't as important as the fact that you create a system around both positive and negative market feedback, which does two things:

1. It shows you expect that both will come, which neutralizes the weight that either will have on you.

2. You've created a framework for handling market feedback, taking the emotion out of it, and turning it into a tool for achieving your goals and realizing your vision.

Bottom line, don't get caught up in what people are saying about you. Listen, but have a productive way to process it without losing sight of what matters.

CHAPTER NINE

* * *

WHO NEEDS SILICON VALLEY?

A CHAPTER ABOUT VENTURE CAPITAL

Venture capital (VC) is the unnatural financial force that has most changed the business landscape over the last 150 years, yet it isn't well understood by most entrepreneurs. Since I'm now in the venture capital business, and so many entrepreneurs think they need VC investment, I thought it deserved its own chapter. I wish someone had explained venture capital to me when I was getting started.

IF YOU CAN'T BEAT 'EM...

My first real encounter with venture capital was with a venture fund manager named Sid Chambless at his office in

2008. Sid runs Nashville Capital Network (NCN), one of the most well-known venture capital firms in Nashville. He was the primary decision maker on whether or not NCN would invest in a company. I was fortunate to have Emma on my resume, because that got me a meeting with him to talk through the idea behind Remarkable Wit.

"Sid," I pitched. "I'm building a team of software developers that will help entrepreneurs get their software built. We will take our payment in both cash and equity. I call it Venture Technology!" Playing this back in my head, as a venture capitalist who has now reviewed over a thousand pitches, I can only imagine what he was thinking.

We were a consulting and labor augmentation business, which right away is not attractive for a venture capital firm because the multiples on a sale of the company aren't high. My business model created risk where none was necessary by accepting equity that could be worth nothing if our client's company failed or never sold. What I didn't understand was that my model made the ventures we were helping less attractive to future investors because a non-committed company (RW) owned equity.

Sid's feedback was that he couldn't help me, and he sent me to talk to some other people in town to figure things out more. I never did what he suggested because I was pissed off that he didn't write me a check. RW never did receive investment from a venture capital firm, but I wouldn't have to wait long before I had my first experience with a VC firm through the next company I was a leader in, Moontoast.

In late 2010, Moontoast completed a round of funding with Charlie Martin's venture firm, The Martin Companies, which gave us about a year of "runway" (which means cash to spend on expenses before we ran out of money). Part of the deal included a requirement that Moontoast hire a CEO from out of town. The Martin Companies determined that Nashville didn't have the experienced leadership at the time to run a business like Moontoast.

This is a typical consequence of taking investment from a VC firm. The VC firm will often have a say in the leadership team, especially if your team isn't very experienced.

The board and the team selected Blair Heavey to be our CEO. Blair was an experienced technology executive from Boston with several successful runs as a leader in venture-backed companies. As part of the deal to bring Blair in, the Moontoast board committed to build an office in Boston. The purpose was to take advantage of the talent pool there and to find other VC firms to invest in the company.

The fine print on the deal was that I would have to move to Boston at least 50 percent of the time to make the deal work. This would be very hard as the father of two children who had recently gone through a divorce and just started a new relationship. The choices were bad and worse. If I didn't agree, we wouldn't have a CEO, and support from the VC would stop. So after some hard conversations with Rachel and my kids, I agreed to the deal.

While this was hard on my family and on me, it wasn't entirely bad. I built relationships in Boston, one of the most exciting technology and venture capital cities in the world. And, I got to pitch a bunch of VC firms.

Blair was well known amongst Boston VC firms for being on two leadership teams that were very profitable for the VC firms who invested. With that reputation, he was able to book a lot of VC meetings for us. The first meeting I went to was with a group called Kepha Partners. Kepha was a new fund that focused on "seed stage and Series A" investments (don't worry, I'll break this all down later).

In the meeting we met with Eric and Jo, the partners of the firm. They were both nice guys. Blair, Eric, and Jo spent the first five minutes catching up on family and how things were going at Kepha and then we dug into our business. Since I was the unknown in the room, I had to introduce myself. I started to tell them about my background and my time at Emma, only to find out they didn't know what Emma was. The tech company that everyone knew in Nashville was completely off the radar in Boston.

Small fish, wrong pond.

I thought to myself, *I'm a complete unknown, but they know Blair, so I'll just let him talk.*

For the next ten minutes, Blair, Eric, and Jo began to speak another language. Words and combinations of letters that sounded like off-brand food products started flying around left and right. "What's the TAM?" "Have you dialed in the CAC?" "Do you have any MMR yet?"

By the fifth acronym I felt like an idiot and started nodding to give appearances I was following the conversation. But I felt a shift in the room.

They relegated me to only discuss the technology. There was no trust that I knew what I was doing or that I belonged in that room beyond my experience as a programmer. That's OK if all I ever wanted to be was a programmer, but I was trying to move away from that. I spent the last three years learning to be a businessperson in the school of hard knocks. The meeting with Sid years before left me disgruntled and obstinate, but the meeting with Kepha Partners made me feel inadequate and was the slap in the face I needed to realize that I had a lot more to learn about venture capital.

> **Note:** Now having spent the last five years working in venture capital, I know that I felt inadequate because VCs speak in code to make the uninitiated feel that way.

Even with Blair's solid reputation, Moontoast never successfully raised any VC money outside of The Martin Companies. I have lots of theories about why this happened, some of which involved our business model, but they can't all be explained this way. One of the reasons we couldn't raise money was because of how VC firms work, and why they invest in the companies they do. Much of it is biased. You can look at the trends in who receives investment by demographics, geographic location, and educational background and see that venture capital is a very biased industry.

Most people in America don't understand venture capital. It's not well documented, and the average citizen can't participate in it because of regulatory restrictions designed to protect people from making investments with risks they don't understand. What we do know is that the most valuable companies of the modern era—Facebook, Amazon, Google, and Apple—were all made possible because of venture capital.

Venture capital was also a big part of the launch of iconic companies like AT&T and General Electric, not just the dot-com companies of the last twenty-five years. Venture capital is a very important part of the business world and this chapter will help you understand it better.

WHAT IS VENTURE CAPITAL?

Venture capital is a method of investing money into businesses that are not listed on the public stock markets. The venture capital business model is to generate strong returns on investments made in privately held companies. It is important to understand that venture capital itself is a business. Once you understand that, you can begin to understand the roles of the people who work in the business.

RISK AND ACCREDITATION

Investing in venture capital is generally restricted to wealthy individuals and families, endowments, pension funds, companies, and banks. Nations all over the world have instituted the concept of an "accredited investor" to determine if someone can handle the risk associated with investing in a venture capital deal. In America, the current qualification for accredited investors is a net worth of $1 million or a history of making $200K ($300K if married) a year for the last two years.

The reason this regulation is in place is that venture capital is very risky. The US government doesn't require audits of companies on the private market as it does on the public market. That means the burden of research or what we call *due diligence* in the venture capital world is on the investor. The government wants to make sure that people who make venture investments understand the associated risks and lack of protections, and can afford to handle the due diligence on their own.

Having managed VC funds for the last five years, I have developed a new level of respect for the risk that venture investors take on. Yes, the rewards can be great for a successful venture capital investment. But investors put their money at significant risk when they make a venture capital investment. It is this risk that defines everything else I'm about to tell you about how venture capital works.

WHERE THE MONEY COMES FROM

I've just explained to you that the money used to invest in private companies in what we refer to as "venture capital deals" comes from accredited investors. This, however, does not give you clarity on who you will work with when you try to raise money from a venture capitalist. Is the person you're dealing with investing their own money? The answer is maybe.

There are some key categories of venture capital that will help you know whose money you are dealing with:

ANGEL INVESTOR

This term is reserved for accredited investors who by themselves are in a "network" of other accredited investors, and make investment decisions themselves. Angel investors usually work with the entrepreneur they invest in because they enjoy being involved in the business. Many times they want to take a role in the company at the point of investment or down the line.

Angel investors are often the first investors that put money into a private company after the founders themselves and friends and family. The world of angel investing has gone from something unsophisticated to a mature industry with best practices, a robust market of operational software, and people who have become professionals in the field. Online tools like AngelList help angel investors find companies to invest in and find other angel investors to coinvest with them. This coinvest process is called "deal syndication." More and more deals are being done by angel investors because the networks to support them and connect them to entrepreneurs are better than ever.

FAMILY OFFICE

When a family has created significant net worth, usually $30 million or more, they need to structure their wealth management like a business. That usually means hiring someone to do that management. That someone could be a member of the family, someone from outside the family, or a firm that does this for multiple families. This scenario is called a family office.

Family offices may be the least understood piece of the venture capital world. Though there are thousands of them in the United States, they aren't listed online. They are only accessible through real-life social networks (think country clubs, not Facebook). Family offices, just like angel investors, aren't likely to only invest in venture capital deals. They also invest in stocks, bonds, real estate, hedge funds, etc.

Note: The variety of investment types I listed brings up a term I want to make sure you understand: asset class. An asset class is a type of investment (also called a security in the investment world) that has a distinct way of being bought and sold, valued, regulated, and managed. In venture capital, even though you invest in stock just like you would on the stock market, it is not considered the same asset class as public company stock. It is not purchased the same way, regulated the same way, or valued the same way, so it is a different class.

Family offices rarely advertise that they are venture capitalists because they are in the business of wealth management for their family. But a good strategy for wealth management is having a diverse group of asset classes in your investment portfolio. This is where venture capital comes in. Venture capital, because it's not as regulated and the chances of a company succeeding are low, is considered one of the riskiest asset classes you can invest in. However, it's also known as one of the best yielding (meaning you get the biggest return on your investment) asset classes you can get into if it works.

There are some family offices where the family made their money as entrepreneurs and in those cases, you may see them promoting their venture investments. This was the case of the Rockefeller family, who managed the net worth generated by John D. Rockefeller as a family office. Their family office became one of the first traditional venture capital firms in the world—Venrock.

Fun fact: Venrock was the first venture capital firm to invest in Apple. The most valuable family of the 1800s was the catalyst for the most valuable company of the twenty-first century.

VENTURE CAPITAL FIRMS

So what did I mean when I said that the Rockefeller family office turned into a traditional venture capital firm? I meant that they went beyond simply managing their family's venture investments and began to manage other people's venture investments. This distinction is where most people unfamiliar with how venture capital works get lost. When people talk about venture capital firms, they are referring to professional money managers, managing many other people's money, not just their own or a single family's.

Venture capital firms are diverse in many aspects:

- The industries they invest in
- The size of the checks they write to companies
- The point in the company's life they invest in
- The geography they invest in
- Whether they invest in products, services, or both

The list can go on and on.

There are lots of things that distinguish one venture capital firm from another. The common thread of venture capital firms is they raise money from accredited investors and manage those funds by making investments in private companies. Their aim is to manage those investments to a successful return for the accredited investors, who are their customers.

LPS AND GPS

There are two key types of partners in a fund. The accredited investor and the fund manager. In VC speak, we refer to the accredited investor as a Limited Partner or LP. LPs are the primary source of capital for a fund. They are the party who the fund manager raises money from and who the fund manager works for as they make investments in companies. The LPs are investing because they believe in the fund manager's ability to generate a return on their investment, period. LPs can be individuals, family offices, or institutions like corporations, pension plans, endowments, or large nonprofits.

You probably guessed that if the accredited investor is the LP, that the fund manager is the General Partner, or GP. It's common practice for the GP to invest in the fund to align incentives, but they are usually not the primary source of capital for the fund. Again, this separates a venture capital firm from an angel investor or a family office: the raising and managing of other people's funds.

There is significance in the terms *limited* and *general*, but let's focus on the difference as it applies to the entrepreneur seeking to raise money. If you go to raise money from a venture capital firm, you will interact with the GP and their staff (if they have one). You will probably not be speaking with the LP, because they hired the GP to deal with you.

If you're an entrepreneur pitching a VC firm, the person you are speaking with is not just investing their money, they are investing their customer's money. They went through the arduous process of raising money from LPs, convincing them to believe they are skilled enough to invest well and produce a return. Often, the GP isn't wealthy. This is a job for them. Just because they are managing tens or hundreds of millions of dollars doesn't mean they are worth tens or hundreds of millions of dollars.

A GP is often an upper middle-class person whose livelihood is on the line based on making the right decisions with someone else's money. If they do well and produce a solid return on investment for their customers, they will live to raise another fund. If they don't, they could very well be out of a job. Being a GP is a job, and their performance matters. And, it's a very hard and risky job. Glamorous? Maybe. Lucrative if successful? Absolutely. But very risky compared to most jobs.

Most businesses fail. Somehow, GPs must attract the ones that are less likely to fail, close a deal with them, and then assist them to a successful outcome. The odds are not in their favor, and a successful outcome is not as clear-cut as it sounds.

HOW RETURNS WORK

"Was it a win for you?"

This is a question often asked in venture capital circles. Often, it's asked about a company that a firm invested in that was acquired. It would seem that if a firm invests in a company, and that company sells, that it would be a win for the firm. Not even close. There is a lot more that has to go right in order for the firm to call it a win.

A "win" occurs when a VC firm receives more money from

the proceeds of a company sale (or refinancing) than they invested in the company. Here are some qualifying questions about a win by that definition:

- How much more money did the firm make from the proceeds than they invested?
- How long did it take to get the proceeds from the date of the investment(s)?
- Did the result match (or exceed) the pitch that the GP made to the LP when they raised money from them?

These qualifying questions are what GPs who run VC firms get paid to focus on and have good answers to. They all relate to how successful the GP is in the eyes of their customer, the LP. And how is success determined? The universally accepted answer in the investment industry is a metric called Internal Rate of Return, or IRR. IRR results from a complex calculation used to determine how valuable a particular capital investment is against other capital investments. You need not understand how to calculate IRR because there are calculators out there that will do this for you. However you need to know that IRR is the accepted metric used to determine how valuable a particular investment is.

Understanding IRR is critical to understanding the VC industry, because it serves as a reminder that investors don't have to invest in venture capital, a relatively risky asset class. Venture-backed companies are usually not a sure thing yet, so there is the standard risk of the business failing when it is attached to the investment. There are very little protections against fraud, and the private market isn't heavily regulated or equipped with analysts helping you be smarter about it as an investor. If an LP makes less money on their investments in venture capital than they do in their real estate and stock investments, why would they invest in venture capital?

GPs raise money by convincing LPs that while venture capital is risky and hard, they are great at it and can produce a higher IRR than other asset classes the LP is invested in. Remember, the only reason most investors put money into venture capital is to get a great return! I have to drill this home because, if you pitch a GP at a VC firm, you need to understand what their motivation is. They are not motivated solely by helping entrepreneurs realize their vision. They have to balance that goal with producing an outsized return for their LPs.

VC firms focus on two things when striking a deal: terms and valuation.

TERMS AND VALUATION

Now that we've exposed the dynamics of the VC firm and understand the GP's motivations, let's talk about how they are compensated.

GPs at most institutional firms are compensated by a model called "2 and 20." This is shorthand for 2 percent of the funds raised in management fees and 20 percent of the carried interest. Let's dig in.

First, the management fees. GPs charge LPs a fee for managing their money. This is not unreasonable. GPs have operating costs (office, administration, travel, etc.), liabilities inherent with managing money, investments that require insurance, and are doing work that they are paid a salary for. GPs generally charge management fees of 2 percent of the total size of the fund for each year that they are managing the fund. Let's play this out.

Let's say a VC raises a fund of $100 million (which is very hard to do). Now let's say they manage that fund for five years. They will charge a fee of $2 million (2 percent of $100 million) a year for five years, totaling $10 million. Even though the fund was a $100 million fund, they will only invest $90 million in companies. If the fund is successful, this seems like a small price to pay. But if not, the LPs will still have paid the GPs $10 million dollars. This is why it's good to be a GP.

Now for the carried interest. Carried interest is a fancy term for profit sharing used in the investment world (I swear we have so many code words, it's ridiculous). Carried interest is the real incentive for success and is where

GPs should be focused in terms of compensation. It creates alignment with the LPs for the GP to earn a percentage of the profits from an investment that was successfully made and managed.

The profit on an investment is not every dollar returned, but rather every dollar above and beyond the initial investment. Simply put, if you invest $1,000 into a company and you receive $2,000 back from the company in total, then you profited $1,000. This profit is the focus of a GP's carried interest. No LP wants to pay a GP a management fee and let them take a percentage of every dollar returned. So it will be negotiated in terms of the fund between the GPs and their LPs what capital must be returned before the GP can begin to participate in the success of the fund.

The standard 20 percent carried interest incentive applies here. Once the initial capital invested by the LPs has been returned to them and any additional liquidation preferences that were agreed upon in fund terms, the GPs will earn 20 percent of every dollar that comes back to the fund. If the fund was a $10 million fund and returned a total of $100 million, we can assume that at least $10 million had to be returned to the LPs. What remains is $90 million in returns. The GPs' carried interest amounts to $18 million. This is why the venture capital business can be so lucrative.

Now that we understand how GPs are incentivized, we need

to cover the work that they do. This can be broken down into four key areas: Fundraising, Selection, Dealmaking and Portfolio Management.

FUNDRAISING

By far the hardest job any GP has, especially when they are first getting started, is raising their first fund. This has all the difficulties of most entrepreneurial endeavors. You have to craft your business plan, set up the framework of your operations, and sell, sell, sell. What is very different than most businesses, however, is that the fundraising phase is in some ways a measure of success. The GPs' work after the fund has been raised is much easier than the work during the fundraising process, and the business model and revenue model are locked in once the fund has been raised.

Because most funds run their day-to-day operations on management fees, the business model will largely be dependent on the size of the fund that is raised, and has implications on the way the fund will handle selection, dealmaking, and portfolio management. If you raise a $100 million fund, you have $2 million a year for five years to operate on. You can hire several people with that kind of budget. These days it's not uncommon to see a $10 or $20 million fund, and now you are talking about just $100-200K of management fees. That is a very small budget for day-to-day operations. That kind of fund has to operate very differently.

Small funds are raised from high net worth individuals and sometimes family offices. Large funds are raised from large net worth family offices and institutional investors like pension funds and endowments. These different types of LPs have different expectations on how their money will be managed and that will filter down to the way the GP operates.

Finally, it is in the fundraising process where the GP generally commits to what kind of investments they will make. This is very important. LPs will not invest in a venture fund unless they understand the investment model that the GPs will use when making investments. This includes important features like what industries the companies are in, what their business model looks like, how mature they are, where they are headquartered, and more. If your company doesn't match those predefined criteria that the GP sold to their LPs during fundraising, then your company is not a candidate for investment, period.

When a GP positions what kind of fund they are raising, they will select a stage from the venture capital segments of investment rounds. There is no universal definition of these stages, but generally they can be categorized as follows:

- **Pre-Seed:** Very small investments from friends and

family, usually angel investors. There are very few pre-seed VC firms.

- **Seed:** The first official professional investment made in the company. The riskiest stage that VC firms invest at. These rounds usually range from $50K–$1.5M.
- **Series A:** This is usually the investment used to grow an early stage business that has a proven business model. These rounds usually range from $1M–$5M.
- **Series B:** This is the round that helps a company scale to meet a growing demand. These rounds usually range from $7M–$10M.
- **Series C (and above):** Once you get to Series C, you are scaling the business. It's already profitable, and now it's time to capture the market opportunity as quickly as possible. These rounds are usually a minimum of $15M.

After fundraising is complete, the GP shifts their activity with LPs to what's known as investor relations. This simply means keeping their LPs informed (usually on a quarterly basis) on the state of the fund.

SELECTION

VC firms spend a large percentage of their time evaluating deals for investment. Ultimately, this is a process of selection. Like all downstream work that VC firms do, fundraising has a significant impact on the way that selection will occur. For example, if the fund is very large and the investment model requires that the maturity of a company must be such that it is generating $30 million in revenue (Series C or greater), this will greatly limit the number of companies that the VC firm can select from. If the fund is small and can only invest less than $1 million in a company (Seed), then the selection process will require the VC firm to look at many more companies, since there are far more startups around that would be eligible for that level of funding.

In the twentieth century, selection in the venture capital business was a "closed network" process. By closed network, I mean that getting your company funded by a VC firm was largely based on who you knew, and those networks often came from university alumni groups, family connections, and even country club memberships. Today, the internet has greatly opened the network by which companies can be selected by a VC firm for investment.

There are more venture firms today than ever before, with a very diverse set of selection practices. For example, some funds are explicitly selecting companies based on the demographics of the founders like gender and race in an effort to both balance the current trends of who gets funded, and take advantage of untapped pools of entrepreneurs who are likely to succeed but more unlikely to get funded. Some funds are using data science to arrive at investment decisions to avoid the biases that humans make in selection. There is a lot of variety in VC firm selection processes today, and we can expect there will be even more in the future, as VC firms continue leveraging technology and getting more niche in their investment models.

DEALMAKING

The magic of venture capital happens in the way the deal is structured. It took me years to understand how important this aspect of the business is and a few more years to be able to distill it down to two key financial areas that anyone involved in a VC deal needs to understand: Valuation and Liquidation Preferences.

WHAT IS A VALUATION?

Valuation is the *process and result* of arriving at the monetary value of an asset. In VC, the asset being valued is a privately held company. Valuation is both the process and the result because the process used to determine the value is the valuation process, and the result is the company's valuation.

A VC firm's goal is to invest in a company at the lowest valuation possible, and sell its ownership in the company at the highest valuation possible, while keeping as much ownership in the company as possible between investing and selling.

How is a privately held company valued? Negotiation. There is no standard that is universally adhered to, regardless of what anyone says. In venture capital, your company is worth what someone will pay for it, not a dollar more or less. There are valuation models in every industry that are used to estimate the value of a company outside of an actual investment or acquisition process, but I have rarely seen those models hold up perfectly when it's time to do a deal.

What often doesn't get factored into these models is *the value of the capital that the venture fund has*. Entrepreneurs want the capital, and there are more entrepreneurs than there are venture funds. In supply and demand economics, the capital VC firm's control is worth more than the dollars they offer to invest. That often discounts the valuation model that entrepreneurs try to propose. In other words, it's a buyer's market.

Occasionally, a company will have multiple VCs fighting to get in the deal. In this case, it's a seller's market and the entrepreneurs have the leverage in setting the price.

PRE-MONEY VALUATION AND POST-MONEY VALUATION

Now for the magic trick called pre-money and post-money valuation.

When an entrepreneur sets a valuation for their company, it is called a *pre-money* valuation. This is the valuation of the company before any investors put their capital in the business. What's important about this is that it sets the price of the equity for the investor.

If a VC firm invests $5 million in a company with a pre-money valuation of $20 million, then the VC firm is buying 25 percent ownership of the company. Assuming that the founders owned 100 percent of the company prior to this investment, they now own 75 percent of the company. This decrease in ownership is called *dilution*. Dilution is not a wholesale bad word, because sometimes it's necessary to bring a partner onboard who can change the course of the company for the better. But dilution means your ownership percentage has decreased.

However, the founder didn't pocket the $5 million in this situation. The $5 million went into the company's bank account for use. Going back to our balance sheet, this $5 million is added to the assets of the company on the balance sheet. Now the value of the company, *post-money*, goes to $25 million. The VC firm still ends up owning 25 percent of the company, so they have turned $5 million in cash to $6.25 million in stock ownership in the company.

That's great, but you can't spend that stock like you can cash. The real work for the VC is helping grow the value of the company, to make it worth $40–$200 million to another company that wants to buy it.

That's not the only job the VC firm has. The VC firm also needs to maintain their 25 percent stake in the company, and that's difficult. Most venture-backed companies seek additional investments between the time the first VC firm invested in them and the sale of the company. In a future round of investment, if the VC firm doesn't invest, then the VC firm's ownership will be diluted.

This could work out fine if the pre-money valuation of the company during the future round of investment is significantly higher than the pre-money valuation that the VC firm invested at. But if the pre-money valuation is only slightly higher, the same, or lower, then the VC firm's dilution is going to result in a loss of value in the investment.

Let's say the VC firm didn't invest in two more investment rounds that the company raised, and due to dilution, the VC firm's ownership share goes from 25 percent to 10 percent. If the company sells for $40 million, then the VC firm could end up only generating a $4 million return on a $5 million investment. That's not a good result, and it happens more often than you'd imagine.

VC firms had to figure out ways to limit risk in these scenarios. I started this section off by detailing the two things

VC firms care about when striking a deal. We just covered valuations, now let's get into liquidation preferences.

LIQUIDATION PREFERENCES

I've set the stage for the problem. For a variety of reasons, a company might sell, but if the stake that the VC firm has is less than the money they put in the company, their investment will stand at a loss. The VC firm needs to protect against the loss. This is done through a *liquidation preference*, which is established when the investment is made. Let's break down this term:

- Liquidation—to convert assets into cash.
- Preference—priority in the right to demand and receive satisfaction of an obligation.

So what do these two words mean when you put them together? When the company is sold, the investors who have the right get their money back before those who didn't put any money in. Therefore, the founders won't get a dime until the liquidation preference is satisfied. This is how VC firms offsets the risk of the scenario we went through.

Valuation and liquidation preferences are the two key financial terms that VC firms focus on. Most entrepreneurs are not experienced in these two areas, and lose when negotiating on these key terms because they don't understand them.

If you enter into negotiations understanding that these are the areas VC firms are focused on, you can have a more productive negotiation and also earn the VC firm's respect by understanding how their business works.

PORTFOLIO MANAGEMENT

The final area of a VC firm's operational focus is portfolio management. This is a broad area that has many aspects to it, but portfolio management really comes down to a single goal: Ensure that the VC firm's portfolio of investments delivers the result pitched to the LPs. Just as selection approaches and deal terms vary greatly from firm to firm, so do the ways that VC firms address portfolio management.

In my experience, portfolio management can be boiled down to two things: insight and influence.

By insight, I mean VC firms want to collect data and information from companies to understand how they are performing. Based on that information, they can make decisions about how to manage their investment in the company. If a company is performing terribly, the VC firm may choose to write the company off or try to sell its shares in the company as soon as possible. If a company is doing great, then the VC firm may want to spend more time working with the company or maybe even invest more money to help grow its value. If the VC firm doesn't have enough insight into the company's performance, it can't make well-informed decisions about how it should manage the investment.

As for influence, this usually comes in the form of a board seat. Usually, but not always, VC firms will want a board seat as part of the terms of their investment. A board seat gives the VC firm governance rights and the ability to influence the direction of the company. This is particularly important if for some reason the VC firm and the management team become misaligned.

As an entrepreneur, this is something you really need to understand. A VC firm's responsibility as a board member is to represent the interests of their LPs, not to help the entrepreneur. In the best-case scenario, these two things aren't in conflict and everyone gets along great. However, in my experience, more than half the time VC firm board seats become a real thorn in the side of a founding management team.

That is the life of a VC. Fundraising, selection, dealmaking, and portfolio management. It's a job. A high-paying job, but a job nonetheless. Understanding this will allow you to be educated in your dealings with VC firms and hopefully establish a relationship that works out well for everyone involved.

VENTURE CAPITAL IS A GAME, AND YOU CAN ONLY WIN IF YOU KNOW THE RULES

There is nothing evil or wonderful about venture capital. It's a business like any other business. Being ignorant to it leads to making it more mystical than it is. It took years of learning by doing for me to figure out what I told you in this chapter. It's not very intuitive. Hopefully this helps you understand how VC firms will think about an investment in your company, should you seek investment from them. Keep in mind, these are the baseline rules of the game. Lots of firms will have innovations on this model, just like my firm Jumpstart does. But this is the baseline everyone is working from.

CHAPTER TEN

* * *

PARTNER UP

A CHAPTER ABOUT COLLABORATION

Entrepreneurship requires an exploration of one's strengths and weaknesses. When you get clear on your goals and achieving them is the priority, you can only come to one conclusion. You'll need partners to make your vision a reality.

Until now, I have focused on stories of failure. There is good reason for that. I have learned far more from my failures than my successes. You'll be happy to know that you have arrived at the arc of the book where I will turn to my successes.

I talked in chapter 3 about how much I admired Emma and the culture that Clint and Will created. Part of what made that culture so incredible was how strong their partnership was. Clint was an incredible writer and Will was a great designer and enthusiastic technologist. They complemented each other well, and that manifested in the way the culture of the organization developed.

I always wanted to have a partnership like that, but I never came remotely close, until I met Vic Gatto.

UNEXPECTED, UNLIKELY AND UNDENIABLE

My partner, Vic, has become one of my best friends, and that is as unlikely as anything I could have imagined when we first met. He's an Italian guy from Boston and I'm a Black guy from New York. In the Northeast US, that's a setup for a shouting match about who has better sports teams. But in Nashville, Tennessee, it turned out to be the recipe for the city's "Odd Couple of Innovation."

I met Vic in 2008 while growing Remarkable Wit. Vic was a partner at a venture capital firm named Solidus, investing in a wide range of companies from healthcare technology to print media. Back in 2008, Vic saw what most venture investors weren't able to. He saw the impact that innovations in technology were about to have on the venture capital industry.

Nashville's venture capital community was not deep in

technology. They were known for growing very successful healthcare service businesses. Vic started looking away from Nashville's experienced venture investors and towards its entrepreneurs and technologists to learn more about this wave of innovation. That led to his meeting with me.

My motivations were different. I wanted to raise money for Remarkable Wit, and Vic had access to money. But it was 2008, and I hadn't codified the Eight Core Concepts yet, much less decoded how venture capital worked. So there was no chance that Vic would invest in me or my business. But, he was honest and upfront about that and kept the door open for us to develop a relationship. I think he saw me more as a technologist than an entrepreneur and that would have been a fair assessment at the time.

What he couldn't avoid was how hard I was working to become an entrepreneur and how that hard work was elevating my profile in Nashville's developing entrepreneurial scene. When Vic began to experiment with new models for venture investing, my hard work earned me a spot as one of twenty people who he reached out to. This was an invitation from Vic to collaborate and be part of something that he wanted to do. It was not, however, a commitment from him to partner with me long-term. It was simply an opportunity for me to get to know him and this thing he was trying to do.

Vic imagined a new kind of venture capital fund. A fund

based on leaning into technology, investing small amounts of money, and supporting the founders in a way unlike traditional venture capital funds did. Through mentorship and working alongside the entrepreneurs, Vic and his group of twenty supporting co-founders got together over beer and pizza and created a *Shark Tank*-like investment club called Jumpstart Foundry.

Over the years, the number of people willing to work nights and weekends with Vic to help him figure out this challenge went from twenty to three:

- Michael Burcham, the Founding CEO of the Nashville Entrepreneur Center
- Chris McIntyre, the then VP of Product for Change Healthcare (a company in Vic's venture portfolio that sold to Emdeon for almost $200M)
- ...and me.

While we all worked well together, Vic began to confide more in me than anyone. After five years of experimentation, it was time to make Jumpstart more than just a side hustle. It was time to separate Jumpstart from its place as a pet project of Solidus to a project of its own. When it was time to do that, Vic needed to secure at least one partner, and he reached out to me.

I remember expecting him to offer me something between

10-15 percent of the company, which was customary for technical co-founders of early stage ventures. But on our phone call where he made me an offer to be his official co-founder, he offered me 40 percent of the company. This was probably beyond what he had to do, but what it communicated to me was just how much of a partner he saw me as. Since that day, I have treated this company as if I came up with the idea first. I wasn't just his technical co-founder, I was his partner, and I needed to do whatever I could to make this company successful.

As we started to work on the company, we spent entire days sharing our respective views on the market. This is where I got a real sense for why we would be good partners.

- *Our backgrounds were complementary, not overlapping.* We looked to each other for strength in respective areas—him in VC and healthcare, me in technology and entrepreneurship. That has been an enduring aspect of our mutual respect for each other.
- *We had similar values.* We would both work late nights and weekends. We both had two boys, so we each understood the challenges the other faced at home.
- *We both had a chip on our shoulder.* We felt like we were underestimated and not valued for the value we could bring to organizations we had been in before.

These things gave us a solid foundation to build on, and

we've been leaning into these three things for the last five years.

Together, we've grown our firm's portfolio to over one hundred companies. It's difficult, nothing grand is ever easy, but it is evolving to become a very successful new model for venture investing. Through good times and very difficult times, the strength of our partnership has enabled us to both put the company first and continue to position it to be successful. Our partnership evolved from acquaintances, to collaborators, to colleagues, to partners, and somewhere along the line we became very close friends.

The most important moments of our partnership have happened in moments of crisis. We have had several of them in the life of our company, and we have emerged from each one stronger. This is because we have both showed a commitment to each other during the crisis and have not pointed fingers and placed blame. I've never felt attacked in my partnership with Vic. Other partnerships that I've had have crumbled under pressure, with the partners blaming each other rather than becoming more unified.

WHY WOULD YOU ENTER A PARTNERSHIP IN THE FIRST PLACE?

This is an important question. Partnering can be a very risky proposition. Partnerships complicate things right away because they create a vulnerability to a venture as soon as we form them. Like marriage is to a family, a partnership is to a business. Dissolving a partnership can often mean the end of the business. Many businesses cannot survive when partners break up.

Also just like a marriage, partnerships are a lot of work. The need to keep communication clear, honest, supportive, and empathetic is ever present. Failure to do so will erode the strength of the partnership. Relating a partnership to marriage should give you pause. If you are already in one marriage, you know how hard it is. Then why would you want to be in another one?

So back to the question, why would you enter a business partnership in the first place? Here are the two clear reasons you should consider:

1. The venture can't be executed without the partnership.
2. The estimated value of the partnership, once successfully executed, outweighs the risk of the partnership failing.

Let's assume you have decided that one of those two reasons is true for you. Well then let's talk about what you need to do to give yourself a fighting chance.

WHO IS YOUR PARTNER?

How do you know the person you are considering partnering with? One thing I find so surprising about people and the partners they choose is how little they know about the people they partner with. I include myself in that category. It's funny how similar the feelings you get in the beginning of a partnership are to the feelings in the beginning of a romantic relationship. There is often an endorphin rush and a state of euphoria that comes with the start of a new relationship. All the promise of what you can accomplish together, how the two of you against the world will be unstoppable. Yup, I've been there too.

But the reality is, it almost never plays out that way. Once hard times hit, how well do you know each other?

When I think about Will and Clint, they worked together for three years at SmallBusiness.com before striking out together to start Emma. As for Vic and I, we met in 2008 and began working together in 2009. We worked together nights and weekends, developing a working relationship and a friendship for six years before going all in. Working with someone for years before deciding to partner on a venture isn't a guarantee for success. But it can help as you will have seen the person in different situations and how they handle themselves.

If you don't have this working experience, I know it may

seem weird, but I recommend doing professional reference checks. You should be open to allowing them to be done on you as well. Part of partnership is fairness and balance, and you should be willing to do anything you would ask your partner to do.

To take it a step further, I'd consider doing a background check and a credit check. If your business is successful, you'll end up in situations where you or your partner will be subject to either a background check, a credit check, or both. You don't want to be surprised by what turns up in the middle of a deal. Better to know on the front end.

50/50 IS HARD

A 50/50 partnership is hard. Not impossible, but hard. I would describe the partnership that Vic and I have as a 1a and 1b partnership. Vic is the CEO and co-founder, I am the president and co-founder. We both have seats on the board. We started as 60/40 partners. While we've both been diluted by investments we've taken, our ownership continues to sit at a three shares to two shares ratio. Together, we still own the majority of the company.

But, Vic is the CEO and the 1a.

That clarity is helpful for everyone, including Vic and me. I'm fine with this. He had the initial idea and the stronger background in venture capital. And he's a little older than me (ha ha). What happens in a scenario of conflict between us is clear. I have a ton of rights, but Vic's authority is greater than mine.

When the partnership is 50/50, the lack of clarity on who's in control can be a distracting thing. It has nothing to do with the vision and values of the company and has little to do with how the partnership should work to best serve the company. But it can give space for unnecessary power struggles. If you need to do 50/50 with your partner, be sure to spend extra time with your attorney going through conflict scenarios and how to navigate through them. Get ready to hear about the "Texas shoot-out" scenario.

PARTNER DATES

I remember being at the Emma office and being jealous of the times when Will and Clint would go off to lunch or coffee together. I always wondered what they were talking about, who they were talking about, wishing I could be a part of those meetings. That probably had a lot to do with me wanting to leave at the end of four years there.

When Vic and I started our partnership, I was reeling from the terrible ending that Moontoast went through and wanted our partnership to be special. I remember Googling "how to stay in sync with your partner" or something like that and stumbling upon a question on Quora. The question was:

"How often does Mark Zuckerberg hold meetings with Sheryl Sandberg in order for Sheryl to update Mark? How long do they last?"

For anyone on another planet who doesn't know, Mark Zuckerberg is the founder and CEO of Facebook, and Sheryl Sandberg is the COO of Facebook.

What's amazing about Quora is that sometimes the person the question is about will actually answer. And this was one of those times. On December 22, 2014, Sheryl Sandberg answered the question:

"Mark and I meet for an hour on Monday morning and then again for an hour on Friday afternoon. We have held these meetings since I joined Facebook almost seven years ago."

This was enough for me. I told Vic that he and I had to meet every Monday and every Friday for lunch. These lunch dates have been invaluable. Sometimes it's just a time to catch up on what's going on with our families. Sometimes it's planning for a board meeting. Sometimes it's figuring out how we will address a crisis. But the beauty of this commitment is we never have to set the meeting. It's always there no matter what's happening at the company. This commitment of time has kept us aligned and mutually supportive in what is one of the most difficult things two people can try to do, launch a company.

I can't recommend partner dates enough. Leaders have to communicate, and when a partnership is in the picture, that commitment to communication starts with the partners.

BRING YOUR BEST

Once you've gotten past the structure, knowing your partner and committing to high levels of communication, the next thing to focus on is doing your part. You are the person in the partnership that you can control. Make sure you do everything you can to deliver for your partnership and also take a supportive posture with your partner.

A benefit of being in a partnership is that if one partner is weak, the other one can step in and help. Always focus on how you can do that for your partner.

PARTNERING IS POWERFUL, BUT NOT TO BE ENTERED INTO LIGHTLY

I'm a huge advocate for partnering, but doing so with clear eyes, a clear intention, and a commitment to put in the work necessary for it to be successful.

* * *

CHAPTER ELEVEN

DIFFERENT IS BETTER THAN BETTER

A CHAPTER ABOUT FINDING AN IDEA THAT WILL MAKE MONEY

Before anyone will pay you money, they have to pay attention to you. In a world with so many options of products and services, being a "me too" company will simply not work. Your ideas are worth nothing if they don't stand out in the crowd, and even then, there has to be a market that thinks they are worthy of attention and money.

SO HOW'D YOU GET INTO HEALTHCARE?

Vic and I had been working on Jumpstart Foundry for five years when, in 2014, we began to contemplate doing it as a full-time venture. Jumpstart was born in 2009 as a *Shark Tank*-style investment group of twenty individuals in Nashville who wanted to support the local startup scene with mentorship and angel investment. Vic was the founder, and I was one of the other nineteen folks who answered his call to get active and make a difference in the startup community.

As you might imagine, trying to create a single vision with twenty passionate people wasn't the easiest thing to do. We agreed to meet once a month, listen to three to five startups pitch and write a check for $15,000 for one of them at every gathering. Additionally, at least one of the group's members would sign up as a mentor for the company that was funded. It was a startup funding initiative that Nashville never had before, and it got us a lot of attention.

After meeting for seven months, we realized that the commitment to gather a quorum of twenty members each month was becoming harder and harder. So was finding solid startups to pitch. For some of our members, Jumpstart Foundry was beginning to feel like a part-time job, and that wasn't what they had signed up for.

Vic and a few other members (including myself) started thinking about how to make Jumpstart more programmatic, repeatable, and scalable. We looked around the country for models and found a group in Boulder, Colorado called

Techstars that had done what we were seeking to do. Like Nashville, Boulder in 2009 was not a hot bed of technology startups. But Techstars assembled a small group of committed investors and entrepreneurs who loved Boulder and wanted to see it become a better place for startups to launch.

When we started studying Techstars, there was one other group in the world operating like them—Y Combinator. Y Combinator was created by Paul Graham, the dot-com programming icon who founded Viaweb and sold it to Yahoo! in 1998, when it became Yahoo! stores. Y Combinator was born in Silicon Valley in 2005, and they invented the model of what we know today as startup accelerators. Silicon Valley is the obvious place for accelerators to be born; it's the undisputed worldwide home of fast-growing technology companies and venture capital.

Techstars, the number two accelerator, was born in Boulder, Colorado, and that made no sense. Boulder is a town known for its beautiful landscapes and passionate, active, outdoor culture, not fast-growing startups. So Jumpstart Foundry had a lot in common with Techstars and we decided to model after them. I reached out to a guy I knew in Techstars' portfolio, Alex White, the CEO of Next Big Sound (which was acquired by Pandora). I asked Alex if he could help us get connected with the Techstars folks. Alex was very helpful and connected us with Techstars' co-founder, David Cohen.

After some quick discussions between our two camps, Jumpstart became one of the first ten accelerators in the Techstars Accelerator Network. That meant we received their entire playbook to build our own accelerator model from. With that, we became one of the first fifty accelerators in the US, and the first accelerator in the southeast. Companies from all over the world applied to be part of the Jumpstart Foundry program. Like Techstars, Jumpstart Foundry provided mentoring, entrepreneurial instruction for a twelve-week program on-site in Nashville, and an investment of $15K in exchange for 7 percent ownership of the startup. It was a lot of fun.

We ran our program in the summer, and in our first year (2010), we had somewhere close to 500 companies apply to Jumpstart. The following year the number declined to about 400. In 2012 that number was cut in half. We were no longer receiving applications from all over the world. In fact, we were now mostly getting applications from the Southeast US.

In year one, companies that applied from overseas were excited about the prospect of moving to Nashville to launch their business. By year four, companies that applied from Knoxville wouldn't agree to move to Nashville for the twelve-week program. Knoxville is only three hours away from Nashville. In case you were wondering, this is not a good trend. To have the best shot at launching great companies, we needed a broad base of high quality applicants excited to work with us on our terms.

Here's the thing…we got better at running an accelerator every year. We improved our training; we got better mentors; we improved our relationships with investors; and we even got better at the application and selection process. In fact, by 2014, an independent ranking was created by researchers at MIT Sloan, and Jumpstart was ranked one of the top fifteen accelerators in the entire country. So why weren't we getting more and better startups knocking on our door?

Remember when I said that in 2010 we were one of fifty accelerators in the US? Well, that number would grow exponentially over the next four years. By 2014 there were over 3,000 accelerators in the US alone, not to mention all the ones that sprung up in other countries around the world. We hadn't changed our terms in five years, and now there were 3,000 other accelerators offering $20K, $30K, and sometimes $50K for the same equity in a company as us. Sometimes for less equity.

Our value proposition went from being unique and valuable to lame and laughable in four short years. We just weren't different enough to be compelling. Nobody needed to leave Knoxville to move to Nashville for the summer to be in an accelerator; Knoxville had their own accelerator. It didn't matter that Jumpstart was a top fifteen accelerator in the country. That wasn't enough of a difference to make people take notice. *Don't believe your own press.*

In 2014 when Vic and I began thinking about working on Jumpstart full-time, we knew we had developed a skill and expertise in identifying and assisting early-stage tech companies through five years of execution. And we knew that even though it didn't matter to the market, we were better than 95 percent of the other accelerators out there because we were more experienced. But how were we going to make a full run at Jumpstart with the market saturation issue? The answer: we had to be different, even if that meant moving into a territory we were not as familiar with. We had to commit to grow.

We began to think about what things we could do that would be defensible as a differentiator. But before we could do that, we had to think about what our vision was in this new, full-time venture. After several conversations, we agreed that creating a **new, predictable way to be successful in early-stage venture investing in Middle America** was the vision. That implied several things. First, it had to be a new and novel concept. Second, it couldn't just mimic what the big venture firms on the coast were doing. So with that, we began to think about what we would do differently.

The first thing we decided was that we needed to invest

more money per company. To break away from the pack of over 3,000 accelerators, we'd need to invest enough money to stand out. We increased our investment from $15K to $150K, but only increased the percentage of the company we would own from 7 percent to 7.5 percent. This makes a big difference to the companies we are investing in and makes a big difference in the types of companies who are attracted to work with us. But an increase in money alone was not enough. That wouldn't make us different enough.

Next, we focused on a unique strength that we had that our competitors didn't have—our geography. Nashville is home to an industry that drives a fourth of its economy: healthcare. Specifically, health systems (think hospitals). Nashville has more headquarters of for-profit hospitals, ambulatory surgical centers, and behavioral health centers than any other city in the United States.

Also, Nashville is a big town but a small city. Vic and I had relationships with leaders at many of the leading companies in the city. This is a distinct advantage to us as investors, but also to the companies we invest in trying to sell into this market. We can't force a large healthcare company to work with one of our portfolio companies, but we can definitely help with marketing and sometimes even with important introductions. This is a big differentiator.

So we made Jumpstart Foundry a healthcare-only, early-stage venture fund. In doing so, we missed out on lots of deals. But we now had a clear, differentiated value proposition for two very well-defined customers, the healthcare entrepreneur and the healthcare venture investor. The healthcare entrepreneur's job is to build their business by producing a product that solves a problem in the healthcare industry and sell that product to their target customer. The healthcare venture investor's job is to invest the wealth they are responsible for managing (their own or an organization that they are responsible to) for a significant return.

It's our job to help our customers do their job.

We grew our team and created an array of services for our portfolio companies that complemented the capital investment we made in them. These were staffed services focused on assisting with business development and growing their connections to other investors.

As we made these changes, we were destined to make mistakes. That's part of innovation. Vic had some prior experience investing in healthcare but neither of us had ever gone 100 percent all in on the healthcare industry. When we first did it, people in Nashville didn't understand the decision and some who loved us for what we did as an accelerator disapproved. We didn't know how we would build all the complementary services necessary. We didn't even know what they needed to be. We didn't know how we would raise enough money to invest ten times what we had done in the past. But the bold vision, our credibility, and a lot of hard work created a path for us to be successful.

Today, five years after making these changes, our team has grown from four people to fifteen. Our revenue grew 1,300 percent and our portfolio value has gone up thirty times. We took a leap in 2014, going from something we were great at to something we had very little idea how to do. But moving towards what is *different and viable, even if not well-chartered,* was responsible for our organization's success and growth.

NAVIGATING BEING DIFFERENT AND ALSO BEING VIABLE

Some things in business are more art than science. Making your business attractive and comprehensible to your customers is one of them. There's a needle to thread. The challenge is to stand out through clear differentiation but also ensure that the value proposition put forth to the market is real. It's easy to say that you have to be different while solving a real problem. But if it was that easy, everyone would do it. There are three concepts that can help you think through your business idea and evaluate whether or not you can thread the needle with it.

SATURATED MARKETS

The nonscientific definition of saturation is "to a very full extent, especially beyond the point regarded as necessary or desirable." Saturated fat was named that because it has too many hydrogen molecules. Eating too many saturated fats has the effect of raising the cholesterol in your blood, which increases your risk of heart disease or stroke. A saturated market is one with too many businesses in it providing the same (or very similar) products and services to consumers. The effect of a saturated market on your business is customers don't need to adopt your offering unless it is very different in value delivered or price. Therefore, in a saturated market, you have a higher likelihood of failure.

Sometimes saturated markets are great markets, because the companies in them have lost the competitive edge in how they treat their customers, produce their products, or deliver their services. These are all areas that a new entrant to the saturated market can focus on in order to stand out and be different enough to be attractive and viable. But beware, saturation is a difficult challenge to overcome for new businesses. If your value or price doesn't strike a stark comparison to the existing saturated market, you are likely to be swallowed by consumer apathy and fail.

NASCENT MARKETS

The word *nascent* means "just coming into existence and

beginning to display signs of future potential." A market is nascent when what you are doing is different from anything the world has seen done at scale. As a venture capitalist, I talk to a lot of founders who are embarking on a nascent market. Nascent market ideas are exhilarating for the person who created them, and for futurists who live with one foot in today and the other in tomorrow. But for the pragmatic marketer, nascent ideas smell like a failure waiting to happen. That's because the burden of educating the consumer about the market is on them.

Peter Drucker is one of the most recognized business minds in the world, having written *Management: Tasks, Responsibilities, Practices*, widely considered the definitive book on management. He said, "The purpose of business is to create and keep a customer." If we accept his statement as true, then we must ask, "What is required to create a customer?"

Depending on your business, the specific answer is likely to differ. What will remain the same is that a customer must first realize a need, then they must desire that need. Finally, they must choose you to fulfill that need. This is the **customer journey**, the path a person takes to become a customer of a company.

In a nascent market, it becomes the responsibility of the company to ensure that the customer is even aware of the need. In a nascent market, the customer is not aware that they have a need at all. We call this process "educating the customer." It takes time and is often very expensive. If you don't have a significant budget set aside for this education process, you are likely setting yourself up for failure.

A lack of awareness about the problem you seek to solve is a sign that customers are uneducated about their options and don't demand new solutions. You can win big in a nascent market, but you have to understand the responsibility you have to educate the market, and be prepared to pay to do so.

SOFT MARKET VS. HARD MARKET

This chapter is about finding an idea that will make money. There are lots of them out there. I'm not here to tell you whether or not your idea will make money. But I want to make sure you understand the market conditions that indicate the likelihood of your idea making money. It's a matter of economics. The saturated market is also sometimes called a soft market in economic circles. A soft market is one where there are more sellers than buyers, and as a result, the buyer has the leverage to negotiate the price down.

A hard market is the opposite and is not analogous to a nascent market as a soft market is to a saturated market. A hard market is one where there are not a lot of suppliers, but there are a lot of buyers. This implies that demand is high. Sometimes people mistake a nascent market for a hard market, but I want to reinforce that they are not the same thing. A nascent market does not have a lot of buyers. If you are reading the tea leaves here, you've already concluded that a hard market is likely a good market to find ideas that will make money.

The key then is to identify a hard market and then understand how it became hard and why it hasn't gone soft yet. Since we are talking economics, let's acknowledge that how most markets move is irrational and happens by a combination of forces that most people cannot predict. Your ability to identify a hard market is related to how well you understand that market and industry.

My example of this is real estate. I am not good at real estate. I don't understand the trends that drive it very well because I've never worked in it. I also don't love it. As a result, when Nashville's housing market became one of the hottest in the country, a certified hard market, I couldn't take advantage of it.

I know the tech startup market very well. As of this writing, I've worked in it for almost twenty years. I've had thousands of conversations about it across the country. When the number of high quality startups continued to soar and funding sources for them did not, we saw the hard market and provided a differentiated offering to serve it. Twice.

Once as an accelerator for a broad hard market, and when that market became saturated and soft, Vic and I evolved to once again be different in another hard market. That's only possible with expertise.

RESPECT THE POWER OF THE MARKET

If this chapter has a takeaway, it is that your business is not about how great your idea is in isolation. It's about how well it is received and adopted in the market. And that has more to do with the market than it does with your idea. It takes discipline to avoid the kinds of biases that will cause your business to fail because you don't respect the power of the market. You are not your market. Your friends are not your market. Be critical of yourself with the facts, focus on industries where you have expertise, and you give yourself the opportunity to identify an idea that can actually make money.

CHAPTER TWELVE

● ● ●

ORCHESTRATE

A CHAPTER ABOUT PULLING IT ALL TOGETHER

The magic starts to happen when your knowledge is complete enough to enable you to get massive things done through communication and coordination. Impact and influence is multiplied when you can get a large number of people to read from the same sheet of music, play their part, and commit to harmony as the priority.

MAJOR ACCOMPLISHMENT

I'd like to tell you the story of the rise of professional soccer in Nashville through the ranks in record time (2014–2018), from my seat.

In 1989 (when I was a freshman in high school in NYC),

Lynn Agee and Devinder Sandhu co-founded the Nashville Metros, a semi-professional soccer team. For almost twenty-five years, soccer struggled to be taken seriously in the United States. Against the more popular American sports of football, baseball, and basketball, the Nashville Metros gave fans in Nashville a soccer team to cheer for and support. In 2012, unfortunately, the Metros' run ended, and Nashville no longer had a team to get behind.

In 2013, a Middle Tennessee native and sports fanatic named Chris Jones (who I'll refer to as Jones) thought it was a shame that Nashville didn't have a soccer team to support anymore. Jones had an idea to rally soccer lovers across the city to band together and form a new club that they, as a community, would own. Jones took to Twitter to share his vision, and in a true testament to the power of social media, a movement was born. Others agreed with Jones and gave him the backing he needed to take the first steps of getting things up and running.

During the day, Jones was a banker at a local bank, Pinnacle. But on nights and weekends, he was building the future of Nashville's soccer supporter community, Nashville Football Club (Nashville FC). Nashville FC was a nonprofit membership group where anyone could become a voting member by paying membership dues, which were around seventy-five dollars a year. The founding members received commemorative scarves and membership cards that gave them access to games, assuming the club ever played anywhere. Hundreds of members signed up, including me, before the club ever had a license to play in any league.

Jones hustled, with the help of his wife and a tight band of people that would become the board of the nonprofit. They turned Nashville FC from a social media following to a reality that would make fans of the Nashville Metros proud. Nashville FC got a franchise from the National Premier Soccer League, a sanctioned US Soccer fourth division amateur soccer league. Less than one year from Jones's initial tweet, Nashville FC fielded a team for competition. On May 24, 2014, Nashville FC played its first ever home match at Vanderbilt Stadium, and defeated the Atlanta Silverbacks Reserves 3–1 in front of 2,000 fans.

Nashville FC earned a playoff spot in its first season and became the darling of lower division soccer fanatics across the country. It would have been incredible if the story ended there, but lucky for Nashville, its soccer fairy tale was just getting started.

At the close of Nashville FC's first season in August 2014, Jones reached out to me. I asked him questions about the business throughout the season, and he finally had a moment to catch up with me and talk about the organization. We had lunch to discuss the future of the club, and Jones asked me to get more involved. He believed the organization had a bright future but needed help with operations. After some conversation, I agreed to join the board as chairman. On September 25, 2014, the Nashville FC board voted to make me chairman of the board and it was official.

I remember the first meeting we had. We established a vision as a group. Nashville FC would rise through the ranks of US Soccer to become a major league soccer club in ten years. That seemed like a properly audacious vision at the time.

My priority was to tighten up the finance and operations of the org. We started upgrading the club's technology, contracts, and other customer management systems. Our focus was on our second season, but that focus would be interrupted just six months into my term. An article published by Nashville's newspaper, the *Tennessean*, revealed a professional soccer franchise from Harrisburg, Pennsylvania was meeting with the mayor's office about moving to Nashville.

Jones and I responded publicly and swiftly in opposition to the idea that an outside club could come to town and push us out of our own market. That public response was then picked up by the *Tennessean* and seen by our entire membership and the mayor's office. Our message? If anyone will bring pro soccer to Nashville, it will be us. Now we had to act on that statement.

The Nashville FC board meetings quickly became focused on how we, as a nonprofit membership group, could go pro. There was no precedent for this happening. We agreed that we needed to get the support of the membership to move forward. We started to survey the members and the sentiment was cautious support. The members trusted us and knew that it was likely inevitable that pro soccer would come to Nashville. They just asked us to keep the lines of communication open and be transparent.

In order for us to go pro, we would need an investor group. I was the most experienced person in the organization at raising money, so I started building out a deck and putting together a narrative. Everyone started to build a list of people to invite to a potential investor event we held at the end of the 2015 season. The club's coach, Kyle Roelke, coached the son of a man named David Dill. David was the president of one of the biggest health systems, LifePoint Health. David came to the investor meeting at Kyle's request.

During that meeting, David leaned in more and more as the presentation went on. By the end of that meeting, there was a 75 percent chance that David would come on board to lead an investor group. What I didn't know was that David left that meeting, got in his car, and called his friend, Chris Redhage (who I'll refer to as Redhage). David asked Redhage if he wanted to work with him on a professional soccer franchise. Chris, a successful healthcare tech entrepreneur (that I wish Jumpstart had invested in) and former pro soccer player said, "Of course, dude!" And with that, we had an investor group.

The next eight months were a blur.

David, Redhage, Jones, and I started spending a ridiculous amount of time together outside of our day jobs, discussing how this would all work, running numbers, and evaluating options for which league we would go with. There were two options. The North American Soccer League (NASL), US Soccer's second division league, and the United Soccer League (USL), US Soccer's third division league. We met with the commissioners of both leagues, and after evaluating them, decided that USL's business model appeared to be more solid. They were on track to be granted second division status by US Soccer if things kept going their way.

We decided on the USL.

The next big task was creating a deal between the ownership group and Nashville FC that would work for all. David often credited the time he and I spent together as a major reason he committed to move forward as the lead investor. He said that he wanted me to come along for the ride with him as part of the investor group. This was an awesome opportunity, but it was also difficult, because I couldn't do that and also be the chairman of the Nashville FC board. I would have to step down and stand with the investor group as we made an offer to Nashville FC to elevate the brand to the professional level. Through some tough conversations, we made this transition.

We wanted to continue to keep the nonprofit in place as a part of the club as owners. There was some precedent for what we wanted to accomplish in the USL. Seattle Sounders, a Major League Soccer franchise, owned a team in the United Soccer League, and granted a percentage of equity in that USL franchise to a supporters' trust. This was perfect, because it meant we weren't creating something new. We could leverage the model that Seattle had already established with USL and propose that to Nashville FC.

The ownership group made an offer to the Nashville FC board to present to the members of Nashville FC. The offer was to purchase the intellectual property of Nashville FC in exchange for 1 percent ownership in the USL franchise. This would only pass if the hundreds of members of Nashville FC voted to accept the offer with the ownership group. The Nashville FC board did an incredible job of managing the communication with the membership and negotiating on the behalf of members. It's hard to believe in hindsight, but things got tense for a bit there through this process. It was just a matter of everyone trusting that everyone's intentions were good.

The vote came, and the membership voted overwhelmingly to accept the deal—96 percent were in favor of the decision.

That set the path for us to make the move. On May 19, 2016, less than two years from the day Chris Jones and I had lunch, the United Soccer League awarded Nashville a professional soccer franchise. The Roadies, Nashville FC's flagship supporters' group led Mayor Megan Barry with chants, flags, and drums into the Bridgestone Arena for the announcement. It was an amazing day.

For a second, let me stop to take stock of what has happened in my life. It's now the summer of 2016. A little over fifteen years prior, I arrived in Nashville with a small family, knowing no one, with everything I owned in a Mazda 626. On May 19, surrounded by my parents, my wife, my two sons, and the entire Jumpstart Foundry company, I got on stage with David Dill, Chris Redhage, and Chris Jones and announced that Nashville had a professional soccer team.

Who cares about all the failures I've lived through until that point? Relentless hard work, clever thinking, and a belief in myself made this moment possible. It was special, it was one of the best days of my life, and it was a day I never could have imagined.

The celebration wouldn't last long.

A day later, Nashville's leading newspaper the *Tennessean* reported that Bill Hagerty and Will Alexander were also seeking to bring a soccer franchise to Nashville. Bill and Will had an incredibly successful run together working for the state of Tennessee. Bill was the commissioner of economic development and Will was Bill's chief of staff. These guys were professionals at bringing big businesses to the state, and they had their eyes set on soccer.

As distracting as this was, we couldn't get bogged down with it. We now had a professional franchise and needed to get our club ready to play in 2018, just a year-and-a-half away. Because of some trademark issues we encountered, we had to change the name of the USL club from Nashville Football Club to Nashville Soccer Club (Nashville SC). We hired our club's CEO from Major League Soccer. Court Jeske was the Vice President of International Business for MLS and was a great hire for our team. Things were moving along, and we finally got a meeting scheduled with Bill and Will.

In that meeting we got a sense of where things were headed. They didn't want to interfere with what we were doing, but they knew something that we didn't. They knew Nashville had a real shot at getting a Major League Soccer team in the next twelve months. Two years prior, I was with the board of Nashville FC and said that we would get to Major League Soccer in ten years. And here were Bill and Will telling us it could happen within twelve months, which would have been three years from that board meeting. It's mind-bending, but these were the guys who understood how to do this, so we had to believe them.

They were in search of a billionaire to lead the ownership group, because that's what was necessary to make the MLS bid possible. That billionaire would be John Ingram. John is the Chairman of Ingram Digital Group. Ingram is a massive name in Nashville. Ingram Industries is one of the most valuable privately held companies in the country. The Ingram family has been a pillar of philanthropy and civic leadership for decades in Nashville, and everybody in the business community at least knew who John was. I actually knew John.

John was an early investor in Jumpstart Foundry. He was a chair of the Nashville Entrepreneur Center, and we sat on that board together. Small world.

John was completely committed to bringing an MLS club to the city of Nashville. John also had a vision that this MLS club would unite the city in a way that nothing ever had before. That vision was aligned with the vision David Dill, Chris Redhage, and I had when we committed to purchase the franchise from the USL. It was also aligned with the vision that Chris Jones had when he got the inspiration to rally the citizens of Nashville to form Nashville Football Club. And although I wasn't there, I believe it was the vision that Lynn Agee and Devinder Sandhu had when they formed the Nashville Metros now thirty years ago.

A great story was hitting its arc. Thirty years in the making, the city of Nashville would have a top-tier soccer team, but one more important thing needed to happen before it could be possible. If this potential MLS team would unite the city, then John, Bill, and Will would have to partner with David, Chris, and I to lead by example.

This wasn't easy. And not because there wasn't a genuine desire to unify, but because the circumstances of the deal were difficult to navigate. A USL team was already in place with a date to start play etched in stone. That team had to be built out immediately. The USL team had three employees. Court, our CEO, Chris Jones, our general manager, and Lucy Gonzales, a young lady who volunteered for Nashville FC ended up being the first marking hire. This team was building momentum for the brand, and Court was building out the rest of his team at light speed.

For John and his team, they were moving one hundred miles an hour up the steep learning curve of Major League Soccer. There were twelve ownership groups representing twelve different cities that would submit applications for four available expansion teams. The cities submitting applications were Charlotte, Cincinnati, Detroit, Indianapolis, Nashville, Phoenix, Raleigh/Durham, Sacramento, St. Louis, San Antonio, San Diego, and Tampa/St. Petersburg. Nashville was at the bottom of the list when the process started, so John, Bill, and Will had a lot of work to do.

For both groups, aligning was a priority, but as you can see, we were all busy. We determined the only way to unite would be to do a merger. What made the most sense to give the MLS bid the best chance for success was to sell John a majority interest in Nashville SC.

If John became the majority owner of Nashville SC, it would strengthen the application that he put forth on behalf of the city. It also assured the developing fan base of Nashville SC that the owner of the USL and MLS teams would be the same, should Nashville be awarded an MLS club.

In March 2017, one year before Nashville SC's USL club played our first match, we announced the merger. Then, as a completely unified front, Nashville showed the rest of the country that it was our clear intention to join the ranks of MLS. The city was already experiencing so much momentum. We were one of the fastest growing cities in the country, with eighty to one hundred people moving to Nashville every day. Tourism was a runaway success, putting up "best year ever" results for six years running. It was as if when the recession hit in 2009 and everyone else took a step back, Nashville never stopped moving.

The Nashville Predators, Nashville's NHL team had their best season ever, going to the Stanley Cup Final in June. Nashville put on a show for the Stanley Cup no one will ever forget. They filled the entire downtown corridor with fans watching the finals. It was an incredible demonstration of the sports city that Nashville is and would be for its new Major League Soccer team.

In the summer of 2017, Nashville hosted two major soccer matches. One was a Gold Cup match between the US Men's National Team and Panama. The other was an International Champions Cup (ICC) match between English Premier League teams Manchester City and my favorite soccer club in the world (that isn't Nashville SC), Tottenham Hotspur. Both matches ended up drawing record crowds for soccer matches in Tennessee. The Gold Cup match drew 47,622 attendees and the ICC match drew 56,232. These results, alongside the merger of our ownership groups, were a major boost for Nashville in the race for a Major League Soccer expansion team.

The final piece of the puzzle however was the need to secure a soccer-specific stadium. Major League Soccer required any team joining this round of expansion to commit to creating a soccer-specific stadium. This is no small task as the costs for such a stadium get into the hundreds of millions of dollars and always require collaboration with and approval from city government. Competing cities with a deeper history of soccer and a larger designated market area struggled to create a path to a soccer-specific stadium. This is where Nashville shined.

Nashville's Mayor Megan Barry had tremendous momentum. She had one of the highest approval ratings ever for a mayor, close to 80 percent. So her support behind the stadium went a long way. John Ingram and the ownership group put together an incredible deal as far as stadiums go. The deal was very competitive compared to every previous stadium deal in Nashville's history and the deals being proposed by other ownership groups bidding for MLS expansion. When the mayor's proposal to Nashville's Metro Council came up for a vote in November 2017, the council voted to approve the $275 million financing package. That was the final piece.

A month later, on December 20, 2017, Major League Soccer Commissioner Don Garber came to Nashville and announced that Nashville would be the **first** city to receive an MLS expansion team.

ORCHESTRATION IS BIGGER THAN YOU

Being part of the launch of a new Major League sports team is a once-in-a-lifetime experience. Very few people will ever get to see something like that from the seat I was in. The number of things that had to go right in order for this to happen makes the probability that it could ever happen near zero. And yet it happened.

Why? Leadership.

Everyone critical to executing this massive project was aligned in vision. From Lynn and Devinder, to Chris Jones, to myself, to David Dill, and Chris Redhage, to Bill and Will, to John Ingram, to Mayor Megan Barry, to the Metro Council, to every person who supported soccer in Nashville for decades. We each may have had a vision for ourselves individually. But our shared vision for the goal of Nashville to become a top-tier soccer city was what we aligned on and agreed to collaborate towards.

Everyone gave up something throughout this process. It didn't play out the way anyone saw it in their mind and thank God for that. None of us could have written the story as perfectly on our own. Nashville's narrative was that we were the underdog, the unlikely choice for an expansion team. But we knew something the rest of the world didn't. We knew we could out-orchestrate our competition.

WHAT ORCHESTRATION REQUIRES OF YOU

Orchestration must be done with intent and commitment. When everything starts, it's just you, and if you're lucky, it will become much bigger than you. In time, the growth and sustainability of the venture may require you to be replaced.

When you start something, you are the leader. You are the head of finance and operations, the person responsible for growth, the head of product, the service leader, the primary salesperson, and the head of marketing. Almost immediately, it will be your job to replace yourself with people better than you in every category. One day you will need to replace yourself, or at least have the option of doing so. Orchestration is how you navigate growth.

The secret to orchestration is understanding how to influence people to become part of something bigger than themselves. It's alchemy. Getting a group of talented people to collaborate and conform to a model you cocreate.

The key to doing this effectively is to convey vision through narrative. We must craft a narrative that is meaningful and resonates with people.

Why does your company exist? If your answer is to make you rich, or even to make the other people there rich, that's fine, but you'll have a difficult time keeping great people.

Why? Because there is nothing unique about becoming rich or starting a company with the purpose of becoming rich.

Any other company can say the same thing. It is not a narrative, it's a goal. And this is not enough.

ORCHESTRATION IS LIKE GRAVITY

Let's look at the most obvious example of orchestration—a symphony. A significant symphony has thirty to fifty musicians in it. You know that a conductor cannot actually manage every musician in the symphony. That's just not possible. A manager can't effectively manage more than ten employees, and even that number is a stretch. Yes, there is middle management present, but that does not produce the unified front that you experience when you watch a symphony perform. That unity comes from a center of gravity created by the conductor.

One of my favorite companies is Salesforce. Marc Benioff, Salesforce's founding CEO, is one of the great entrepreneurial minds of our time. He has built a massive company that continues to grow and scale its impact on the business world across all industries.

Every CEO has a strength, and Marc's is orchestration. There are two images synonymous with Salesforce. The company's logo, which is the word "Salesforce" superimposed on a cloud, and the other is the word "Software" with a ghostbuster symbol over it. These two images represent the narrative of Salesforce and why the company exists.

First the logo. Salesforce was the first enterprise cloud company. Marc embedded the cloud in Salesforce's logo to ensure that everyone understood that Salesforce was a cloud computing company. You would engage with Salesforce's technology via a browser in the cloud, without exception.

As for the ghostbuster "Software" image, this was the company's clear statement on who the antagonist in their narrative was. Salesforce develops software so they couldn't mean ALL software. No, what they were talking about was "installed software." They were waging a war against on-premise software that required a company to maintain their own servers and deal with expensive support costs. With Salesforce, you would never have to worry about this. Salesforce was always in the cloud, and all the support costs were on their end. You just paid for access to their cloud.

Salesforce grew to be one of the biggest technology companies in the world because they are more than a company, they are a movement.

ORCHESTRATION CHANGES YOU

The opportunity to be part of something obviously bigger than you will change you. It will show you how vital you are, and it will humble you to know how much you need others to do big things. It takes tremendous self-confidence and a willingness to let others shine to orchestrate. But when you get here and you accomplish the thing the old you never thought possible, you'll never be the same.

CHAPTER THIRTEEN

* * *

THE PEAK IS NOT THE PEAK

A CHAPTER ABOUT SUCCESS

The problem with goals is once you achieve them, you go to sleep and wake up the next day without them. Accomplish enough things, and you'll learn to trade your goals in for your practice.

HEAD DOWN, KEEP CLIMBING

I met my wife, Rachel, in 2009 right when Remarkable Wit was being forced to fold into Moontoast. Frankly, I was a mess, and she was a saint to put up with me through that process.

Shortly after meeting her and deciding that I wanted to make a run at a real relationship with her, I had to commit to regular travel to Boston for Moontoast. This was very challenging for us so early in our relationship. Neither of us was equipped for a long-distance relationship. I was still early in the process of a divorce from my ex-wife and working out what it meant to co-parent. Rachel was young, had recently gotten her MBA from Vanderbilt University, and had her entire life and career in front of her. The prospect of becoming a second wife and stepmother wasn't an easy one for anyone to choose.

For years I would medicate the trauma of a failed marriage and other difficult life experiences with drinking and working. Fighting to find a person inside of me worthy of this woman I was so lucky to meet. I was in there, but I was a bit of a mess. She hung in there with me, and bit by bit, I got better. Healthier. More clear-headed. It is still a process. Each day, I feel like I'm becoming a truer expression of who I really am. So much of that has to do with the journey she has allowed me to be on with her.

Have you ever climbed a mountain?

I hadn't until Rachel and I went on our honeymoon in May 2014. I was thirty-eight, had two teenage children, had been through a divorce, and was now beginning my second marriage. I had experienced so many highs and lows that I thought I had a real handle on what life was about. That changed when Rachel and I went to Bali for our honeymoon. We never talked about it before, but once we got there and really got settled in, she asked if I was up for climbing a mountain. I was really only in the mood for relaxing, but it was our honeymoon and she wanted to do it, so I said yes.

On the day of the climb, we woke up around 3:30 am to meet our driver and start the hour-long drive. It was May in Bali and the weather was incredible. I was wearing what I would wear for a long run—shorts, running shoes, and a track jacket. Rachel had a few more clothes on than I did, but not much. We were ready.

We headed out to climb Gunung Batur. Gunung means "mountain" in Indonesian. Batur is an active volcano that last erupted in 1963. I didn't know that until I got to the base, but it made the climb really interesting. We were in a group of eight tourists, led by two young men who climbed this and every other mountain in Bali hundreds of times. We started to make our way up.

The climb was easy. Batur is about 5,600 feet high, and not very steep anywhere. It was a great mountain for tourists, because it felt like a long hike. As we made our way to the top, we could feel ourselves becoming more aligned with nature and more removed from the world below. There were groups of monkeys that were joining us for stretches of the climb, expecting bits of bananas that we would drop for them as we made our ascent. The views became more and more breathtaking with each level we cleared.

There were four significant lessons for me on this climb that extended beyond mountaineering. If you've ever climbed a mountain, you've probably learned these lessons yourself.

The first lesson was that the **peak is not the peak.** When we got to the top, it was an incredible feeling. Hours of moving forward and up to reach the plateau of the mountain, being so close to the clouds and seeing the island from that elevation was incredible. But what you could also see from there was Gunung Agung, Bali's highest mountain (which is also a volcano and erupted in 2018). Agung is almost twice as tall as Balur, and also much steeper. It's also Bali's most sacred mountain, being home to its largest Hindu temple.

Rachel and I realized that we accomplished something great, but that accomplishment made us realize there were opportunities to experience and achieve at a higher level. We spent most of our time at the pinnacle of Batur marveling at the sunrise, but for a bit, we shared the dream of making the journey to climb Agung. There is always a taller mountain to climb. Once you get to the top of one, your views change, and you can see and understand the taller one.

The second lesson was about the change in temperature. Remember that I was wearing shorts and a track jacket?

Well when we got to the top, I was freezing. The weather is different at the top of a mountain than it is at the base. Yes, I know that's logical. What's funny is that when we were preparing for the climb, we were thinking about what the weather was like at the base. We were not preparing for what we would encounter as we successfully arrived at the top. **The air is different at the top**. Most of us never think about that, and that's because we don't spend enough time being mentored. It's true in life, and in business, that the air is different at the top.

The third lesson was **that it's harder on the way down than it is on the way up**. The climb challenges your muscles, the descent challenges your joints. After descending Gunung Batur, I had to give up long-distance running for a couple of years because I didn't understand how to descend and protect my knees. I weighed 245 pounds, so physics wasn't my friend when I brought all my weight down at jagged points for 5,600 feet.

The shock from the descent that day has lived with me to this day. I took cracks to the cartilage in my knees, and while I still can do most things, long-term shock to my knees isn't one of them. These journeys of ambition can bring with them long-term trauma. Don't be surprised by that. I should have been wearing hiking boots that would have absorbed the shock; instead, I wore running shoes. Tools matter. Preparation matters.

> Note: I've adjusted well to life after long-distance running. I've moved onto strength training, mobility work, and martial arts. We can become better and stronger despite our past trauma. I believe it's one of the most important skills we can develop in life.

The final lesson from Batur is that **fatigue is inevitable**. We went back to the resort after the climb, ate a big meal, and slept through the day to the next morning. We were super sore the next day and did nothing but lie around the resort. It wasn't the plan to do that, but it was all our bodies would allow us to do. Being at a resort in the heart of Bali is a great place to experience with severe fatigue, but we aren't always that lucky. Sometimes our journey takes it all out of us and the fatigue sets in at a very hard time and place.

There are and always will be times when recovery and healing is the priority. Expecting fatigue and building recovery and healing cycles into your plans only results in greater longevity and superior performance on your path of achievement. It's simply about respecting your body and your mind and having a real understanding of what you are asking them to do.

In 2016, our friends Jack and Adair, who met at our wedding in 2014 and got married a year later, invited us to Seattle for a Labor Day climb. This time we would ascend Mount St. Helens. I was a much wiser climber this time. I knew that it would be colder at the top. I knew that it would be harder on the way down. I knew that I needed to train for the climb to prepare because it would be steeper than Batur was. Mount St. Helens is almost 8,400 feet high at its pinnacle.

With the experience of Batur fresh in my mind, I picked up a couple more lessons on this trek up the venerable St. Helens. First, the terrain changed on the way up. It started as forest. Then changed to large boulders. Then jagged rocks. Then shifting sands as we made our way to the very top. **There were levels.** What got us through one level would not get us through the next level. Our tactics had to change, and we had to learn new tactics at each level like a child to make progress. *We had to embrace the change and the need to learn our new environment.*

My experience from scaling Batur would prepare me for a successful climb, but it wouldn't spare me any of the realities of the experience, good and bad. As magical as being at the top of Batur was, it could not have prepared me for what it was like to be at the top of Mount St. Helens. That was an otherworldly experience. I felt like I was in the heavens and having done that with Rachel and our friends was a moment I will never forget.

And yet, as we stood at the top, our friend Jack pointed to Mt. Adams. Adams appeared as a greater god looking down on St. Helens, at a height of almost 12,300 feet. Jack started telling us stories of the chasms that one has to cross via a ladder to make it to the top of Adams. I was just starting to feel like an accomplished climber, but Jack provided some helpful perspective. **The peak is not the peak.**

And that brings me to the final lesson of that day that only in reflection did I really come to appreciate. That's Jack. Jack was our guide for the day. Jack grew up in Seattle and grew up in those mountains. Climbing them, skiing down them, and learning their personalities. He scaled St. Helens a couple of times before, so he knew the path.

I took that for granted that day, but it's likely we wouldn't have made it to the top had it not been for Jack showing us the way and preparing us for the challenges that we would encounter at each level. Jack, as our guide, showed us the way, but he couldn't climb it for us. Rachel and I earned that view at the top, but Jack's guidance was critical. **You have to do the work, but it sure helps to have a great guide.**

YES, THE MOUNTAIN IS A METAPHOR

Success is in the eye of the beholder. The way we view success has a lot to do with how we see ourselves. If success is about a moment, that first step on the top of the mountain, then I believe it to be fleeting and maybe even an illusion. Just as you seek to drink it in, when you look up, you see that next peak. It's always there.

The healthiest way to view success is as a commitment to the process. There will be moments of failure, but we can see every step along the journey as a success. And I think this is a much truer view of what success actually is. None of us knows when our lives will dramatically change, or even end. All we have is the moment we are in and our hopes for the future. We need to find success in each moment and let those moments build into our life-long vision.

Don't set the vision as a single success, ignoring all the incredible moments you have on the way there. The peak is not the peak.

I'm submitting this manuscript to my publisher on February 11, 2020. I committed to write this book in the summer of 2015 via a Kickstarter backed by over 300 people who supported my vision to complete it. I thought I would have been done in eighteen months. I didn't know the mountain I was climbing. It has been a great teacher and challenged my view of myself as a success. I knew if I could stay alive, I would find the path to complete it.

I met my guide, an author named Claire Gibson in 2016, who helped me frame the book into chapters with structure, a narrative, and a target word count. Claire was a perfect guide. She believed in me and my ability to get here, but also never made light of the work I was embarking on. I could have used her before I set out to write this book, but who knows, that might have scared me off.

There was a point in 2017 when I sent Claire the book and said, "That's it, I'm done, go through it, help me clean it up, and let's get it out." About a week later I got an email, maybe the hardest one I've ever gotten, that said, "Just keep writing." She could guide me, but she couldn't climb the mountain for me. Painful truth.

Committing to the process is the success.

In 2000 when I first arrived in Nashville, you could not have told me that in eighteen years, I would be a pro sports team owner. I didn't know what a venture capitalist was. I couldn't imagine writing a book anyone would find valuable. I couldn't fathom being married to someone different who has made me a better person and would make my kids her own.

That guy just needed to get out of that efficiency hotel.

Back then, that was the peak. One peak at a time, committing to the process is the success.

ENJOY THE JOURNEY

You are not your last venture or relationship. In the last

ten years I've co-founded eight ventures. Four are still alive, four are dead. Today, I'm only leading one of them, Health:Further. Jumpstart Foundry and Nashville Soccer Club are still climbing. This is my portfolio of work for the last decade. It is not me though. In fact, I couldn't feel more at the beginning of my journey.

The path of the entrepreneur often extends beyond a single venture. I've launched a digital media business, a software development shop, a social marketing platform, a video production company, and more ventures that I didn't mention in this book. All of those companies are now dead. But I carry the lessons from those businesses with me today, and they continue to make me a better entrepreneur and a better person.

The act of pushing forward as an entrepreneur through failures is important. Very few people get it right on the first try. I've talked to many people who say they tried to do a venture and then it didn't work so they went back to corporate America. There is nothing wrong with that, but *it's not possible to leverage the lessons from that prior failure into your next venture if you never do a next venture.*

Through each failure I've had there were damaged relationships, lost money for investors, lost jobs, lost value created. Lots of loss and trauma. And yet I'm still here, forming new and better relationships, making money for investors, creating jobs, and creating value. Those failures are not fatal, they are developmental. Your consistent commitment to your development as an entrepreneur will use all the painful stumbles you go through on your path.

Be present for every up and down in your journey and trust in the Hustler, Hacker, Hero values.

Put in the work, every time.

Leverage your experience and your talents to be clever in all that you do.

Believe in yourself, especially when it seems there is little reason to do so.

Good luck on your journey, my friend. Enjoy every peak.

ACKNOWLEDGMENTS

My deepest gratitude for the support and patience of the Kickstarter backers of this book. You hung in there with me and I will always be thankful to you for that.

Max Goldberg, Kiwi Carranza, Jose, Jon Shearer, Chris Bowring, Ryan Rowland, Foxtrot Games, Kim Vigsbo, Tamara Fyke, John Prather, Connor Walker, Laurie Cumbo, Nicole K. Maholic, Stephanie Forsberg, Nick Caprioli, Jonathan Eisen, Samuel Steele, Jeffrey Box, Duaine Oen, Kate Read Ezell, Deb Kowalski, Patrick McCabe, Ryan N. Olsen, Gina Rinderle, Phoenix, Stephen Zralek, David Allen, Geof, Susan Culkin, Alexandra Sortino, Douglas Ryan, Manuel Zeitlin, Aron Lindegård, Tamara Rogers, Dee, John Hawes, Veer Hossain, Jeremy Breece, Mike Marsalisi, Lee Farabaugh, David Shifrin, Emilie Goulet, Northern Imagination, Ellen Lehman, Nathan Taylor, Justin Levenson,

Matt, James Held, Xavier Jenkins, Alex Najarro, Pat Halper, Jeremy Kane, Mohamed Hassan, Michael Davenport, Steve Repetti, Clint Smith, Samantha K., Angela Wiggins, Kevene L. Harris, Chance Garcia, Matt Roman, Jody Lentz, Dan Roseblade, Brenda Long, Raanan, Steven Drypolcher, Joe Varga, Dreaming Isis, Alice Randall, Todd Sattersten, Nick Ogden, Lim Yuan Sheng, Chris McMurtry, Megan McCrea, Bryan Calhoun, Mary Falls, Salem Bin Kenaid, Ryan Snyder, Casey Tebeau, Christopher Gordon, Angela Rainsberger, Thomas Ward, David Thompson, Syb Bennett, Hermen, Afiba Fairnot, Betsy W Jones, Tim Putnam, Ronald Figueroa, Tristan Whitney, Michael Rustici, Timo Kurz, Dmytro Maly-monenko, Ken Gay, Melissa King, Katie Studley, Chris Schultz, Tom Melchior, Stephen Green, Jim Reams, Joe Storey, Robert A. Goldstein, Nicholas Dunne, Hal Cato, Jonathan, Kwame Henderson, Andrew Vogel, Jessica Waut-let, Shawn Bailey, James Todd, Kelvin Ng, Corina Grande, Jayme Hoffman, Andy MacGillivray, Justin Mooneyhan, Conner Haines, John R Colon, Jan Rivkin, Corey Unwin, Debbie Frank, Christine Bingham, Kevin Brown, Brian Ferry, Jessica Harthcock, Dennis Lyftogt, David Servodi-dio, Perry Peguillan, Tyler Kaftan, Pinky Gonzales, Amanda Cates, Reno Bo, Rashina Bhula, Nick Hiter, Jacob Hall Gordon, Johnny Shoaf, Jaice DuMars, Gail Perry Johnston, Jason Myers, Travis Swicegood, Bryan Jackson, Drew Hart, Will Weaver, Daniel Levin, Erica Wingo Newcomb, Justin Rearden, Lindsey Jackson, John Hare, David Hooper, Jeff Heeren, Phil Cobucci, Evan Light, Robby Macdonell, Robert

Brown, Juan G. Colon, Jason Egly, Joshua Camp, Rebecca Green, Josh Mock, Jon Lee, Alexander Poston, Guy Kopsombut, Jamin Guy, Erin O. Anderson, Catching All Fades, iV, David Beronja, Kelly Hoskins, Robert Hartline, Marcela Gomez, Julie Caldwell, Kay Pfeiffer, Jennifer Gilligan Cole, Kim Hatcher, James Ellis, Kristine LaLonde, Angus Nelson, Logan Buerlein, T. Scot Clausing, Eric Satz, André Kishimoto, Mark Coluccio, Jessica Laura, Paul Schatzkin, jeff obafemi carr, Carla K. Nelson, Patrick Spear, Joyce Lavery, Cameo Carlson, Haley, Sean Tilson, William Barnhard, Francisco Estrada, Page Thompson, Greg Greenwell, Jim Schorr, Deborah Winder, Alex, Howard E. Bolden, Santosh B R, Tyler Willis, Jessica Hill, Scott Greer, Craig Taylor Brown, Robbie Goldsmith, Aaron Beck, Ron and Barbara Winder, Benjamin Goldberg, Katie McDougall, Catherine Oliva, Henri Bailey, Nicholas Holland, Patrick Altman, Maalek Marshall, Joe Stewart, Marcus Hooper, Curt Hahn, Stephanie Teatro, Greg Thornton, Doug Marrs, Darek Bell, Geoff Smith, Jack Rutledge, Jocelyn Harms, Chris, David McKnight, Grant Ford, Naveen Jain, Nicole Maynard, Eric L. Hansen, Donovan Evans, Karen-Lee Ryan, Jose Gonzalez, Tari Hughes, Shelby Brown, Jeff McLaughlin, Chip Petree, Colleen Hopkins, Jim Schmidt, Anthony Ware, Matt Cronin, Chris Blanz, Mark Dunkerley, Adam Solesby, Christopher Parks, Les Gebhardt, Forrest Galloway, Aaron Hartley, Len Prieskorn, Thomas Bernstein, Brent Taylor, LeShane Greenhill, Zain Syed, Kimberly Lexow, Barry Silver, Heather McBee, Doris Wasserman, Steve Berneman, Glenn Acree, Molly Secours,

DeVaris Brown, Stephen Glicken, John Kepley, Rachel Marie, Jennifer, Henry Irvin, Dacari Middlebrooks, Heather Corts, Jon Robertson, Parker Gates, Casey Summar, Melanie Moran, Martha J. Moore, Ryan Macy, Daniel Hightower, Robby Towns, Michael Hart, Brian Wrightson, Helen Darby, Justin Joseph, Alex Ezell, Sadiqua Hamdan, Lindsay Jamieson, Neil Corman, Don Leyrer, Jeff Snyder, Marius Stålby, Van Tucker, Gavin Ivester, Jay Johnston, Avery Fisher, Max Abrams, Artiphon, Matt Phillips, Stephanie Pruitt Gaines, Nan Flynn, Laurie Kalmanson, John Wark, Tori Hughes, Adam Auden, Michael T Baker, JohnPaul Bennett, Ben Ramsey, Michael Woolf, Chris Hefley, Julia Polk, Anony Moose, Fallon Wilson, Hana, Tim Petrikin, Jessica Peoples, Bradley Spitzer, Jennifer, Scott Gordon, Chris Ferrell, Ariel Hyatt, Seth Steele, E. Andre Poole, Brittany McGhee, Kate O'Neill, Eric Brown, Henry Pile, and Jacob Jones.

Extra special thanks to those backers who put a little extra into this effort:

Stuart McWhorter, Sam Lingo, Jason Moore, James Soto, Shana Goldstein Mackler, Lance Kelly, Larry Bernstein, Heather Corts, Jay Lawson, Patrick Rollo, Sara McManigal, and Carl Haley.

To my sister from another mother, Jill McClure, your gift to my dream of this book is something I can never repay. I love you so very much.

To Jacob Jones, thanks for being the first believer in this book and for helping bring it to the world.

To Claire Gibson, thank you for showing me just how hard writing a book is, and for framing up this book for me. And for listening on that one very dark day.

ABOUT THE AUTHOR

MARCUS WHITNEY is CEO and founder of Health: Further, a strategic advisory firm working with leading healthcare organizations, as well as founding partner of Jumpstart Health Investors, the most active venture capital firm in America focused on innovative healthcare companies. He is an in-demand speaker who hosts a podcast called *Marcus Whitney's Audio Universe*, and sends out a weekly newsletter called "Two Worlds." Marcus has been listed in the Upstart 100 by *Upstart Business Journal*, Power 100 by *Nashville Business Journal*, and has been featured in *Inc.*, *Fast Company*, and *The Atlantic*. To connect with Marcus or receive his weekly newsletter, visit www. MarcusWhitney.com.